Follow The Forage For

BETTER BASS ANGLING

Volume 1 - Bass/Prey Relationship

A Guide to Understanding Feeding Activity
and Improving Your Catch!

by Larry Larsen

Book I in the Bass Series Library

A LARSEN'S OUTDOOR PUBLISHING BOOK
THE ROWMAN & LITTLEFIELD PUBLISHING GROUP, INC.
Lanham • Chicago • New York • Toronto • Plymouth, UK

Published by
LARSEN'S OUTDOOR PUBLISHING
An imprint of The Rowman & Littlefield Publishing Group, Inc.
4501 Forbes Boulevard, Suite 200, Lanham, Maryland 20706
http://www.rlpgtrade.com

Estover Road, Plymouth PL6 7PY, United Kingdom

Distributed by National Book Network

British Library Cataloguing in Publication Information Available

Library of Congress Cataloging-in-Publication Data Available

Library of Congress 88-92905   Volume 1

ISBN: 978-0-936513-03-4 (paper : alk.paper)

♾™ The paper used in this publication meets the minimum
requirements of American National Standard for Information
Sciences—Permanence of Paper for Printed Library Materials,
ANSI/NISO Z39.48-1992.

Printed in the United States of America

DEDICATION

To my parents, Floyd and Edna Larsen, for sharing with me their love of fishing and the outdoors. Their encouragement and support through the years is deeply appreciated.

ACKNOWLEDGEMENTS

The author wishes to acknowledge the kind assistance of Lynn and Doug Hannon for their help in reviewing the manuscript, and of Dan and Betty Thurmond for their help in developing underwater photographs for this book. Thanks go to Cliff Shelby for his imaginative illustrations and valuable assistance in cover layout.

I appreciate the cooperation of fishing partners, guides, and professionals over the years which have enhanced my knowledge of the bass. Special thanks to the late Guy Settlemeyer for being the best fishing buddy a man could hope for. Lastly, my appreciation goes to the many magazine editors that I have dealt with over the past 12 years, who have helped me in the writing craft.

PREFACE

Most books written on catching bass deal with selecting proper tackle, finding structure, and then, trying to catch bass regardless of whether or not they are feeding. Submerged structure is important, as is good quality equipment to handle the fish an angler catches. But, the most important key to catching several good bass is finding them in a feeding mood.

This book is written on the basic assumption that bass do feed to survive and grow, and that it is easier to catch a feeding fish than one that is not. I feel that knowing where the bass forage exists will give me a chance at finding more bass.

I have tried to explain where the predominant forage of the black bass can be found, why it is there, and how the angler can be successful in catching a few bass from that area. In this book, I have considered most of the major foods of the freshwater bass. The diet of a bass depends largely on his environment. He is adaptable to that particular habitat where he lives.

Bass will eat about anything, and knowing the whereabouts of the major bass forage in specific waters is the beginning of successful angling. This book should be a learning experience for the amateur and the professional. Hopefully, it will create in the angler, an awareness of forage and of the response of their predator, the bass.

A stomach content analysis may reveal the forage and the angler knows where he caught the bass. This book attempts to pattern the feeding activity and improve the catch.

CONTENTS

THE AUTHOR AND HIS BOOK

In 30 years of fishing, Larry Larsen has literally covered the global range of bass in their pursuit. He has caught limits of bass, ranging from Lake Lida in Minnesota near the Canadian border, southward 3,500 miles to Lake Yojoa, Honduras in Central America. His relentless pursuit has extended across the hemisphere as far east as Cuba's Treasure Lake, and westward 6,000 miles to the plantation lakes in the Hawaiian Islands.

Larry Larsen's angling adventures and research on the black bass have been extensive throughout the southern and midwestern states. He has served as a guide on several waters in Florida and in Texas and currently lives on Lake John in Lakeland. He fishes almost daily and has caught and released well over 100 bass exceeding 5 pounds, primarily on artificial lures. His personal best largemouth weighed over 12 pounds and the top lunker hauled over his boat's gunnel hit the scales at 15 pounds, 3 ounces. In 1982, Larry Larsen established an official line-class world record, certified by the National Freshwater Fishing Hall of Fame, for the Suwannee bass.

Writing about bass fishing for some 17 years, Larry Larsen has studied all aspects of the fish and the ways to catch them. The author is the Florida editor for "Outdoor Life" and bass fishing editor for "Petersen's Fishing" and "North American Fisherman." He is a frequent contributor to "Sports Afield," "Field & Stream," "Bassin'," "Florida Sportsman" and numerous other national and regional outdoor publications, and has more than 900 published articles to his credit.

Larry Larsen's photography has appeared on the cover of many national publications. He has been honored with several awards over the years for his outdoor writing and photography and is a member of the Outdoor Writers Association of America and the Florida Outdoor Writers Association. He is a graduate of Wichita State University and has attained a Master's Degree from Colorado State University.

Very few other professionals in this country have written more on the bass. His writings detail highly productive fish catching methods and special techniques. He believes in explaining to readers the latest and very best tactics to find and catch bass anywhere. The basis of bass foraging and fishing success is presented in this book, as an extention of that philosophy.

The principles explained in this book will help the novice or weekend 'expert' catch more and larger bass from reservoirs, lakes, rivers, or small ponds. The book details a complete system to go about catching America's most popular game fish.

I.
THE PREDATOR/FORAGE
RELATIONSHIP

INTRODUCTION
Foraging Factors and Influences

CATCHING HUGE BASS is not luck and neither is catching big stringers of fish. Of the four largest bass ever caught in this world, three were captured on live bait. The current 21 pound, 3-½ ounce California state record succumbed to the presentation of a crayfish while the previous mark of 20 pounds, 15 ounces was caught on a live nightcrawler. Florida's state record largemouth of 19 pounds was taken on a live eel.

If you cannot see a trend in that, look further at evidence provided by the greatest successful foragers in the aquatic world, big bass. Largemouth bass over 15 pounds are rarely caught, but when they are, the successful angler has probably used either live bait or lures which very closely resemble food that is commonly found in the forage base. Seven or eight states can hold claim to fish of such proportions, but only California and Florida produce such lunkers on a regular basis, totaling maybe a dozen or so each year.

Checking the records of catches in these states will reveal that all behemoth bass were caught on live bait (e.g., crayfish, native shiners, etc.) or on forage facsimiles (e.g., 13-inch plastic eels, "rainbow trout" painted diving plugs, injured minnow lures, etc.) To catch bass, particularly big bass, the best bait should be something the predator can easily identify with, its prey.

It is feeding habits of bass and our knowledge of what appeals to them that puts bass in the boat.

This book is written not to attempt to change an artificial lure tosser into a shiner angler, or vice versa. The intent is to make anglers aware of the extremely important aspects of how the forage base in a lake or river affects angling success. The predator/forage relationship is the most significant influence on bass behavior and your abilities to catch the quarry.

Trout anglers have been successfully "matching the hatch" for years, but until recently, seldom did bass anglers really consider the predator/prey relationship as they picked up a lure. The fly rodding 'purists' will deter-

The successful angler has probably used either live bait or lures which very closely resemble food that is commonly found in the forage base.

mine what the trout are currently feeding on and select a fly that closely imitates the look and action of that insect. Even astute bass anglers, on the other hand, will choose a lure patterned generally after a bass forage without regard to the many parameters which would effect the water's particular predator-forage relationship.

Knowing the effects of various parameters and relating to them will help put more bass on the stringer. Without the proper tackle and the knowledge to use it successfully, the lake bottom could be covered with bass which would never see the inside of your live well. Figuring out what to throw and how to present it correctly is the key.

Bass are voracious, opportunistic feeders which utilize a wide range of forage. Like most predators, they have a large mouth and an elastic stomach. Bass will actively hunt and capture their prey. At times, they will lie in wait and hit at anything that gets near, whether it be a fish, bird, insect, or reptile. I was watching a butterfly flit along a bank about two feet above the surface of a small canal recently when a small two pound largemouth burst into mid-air after the prey. He missed.

Predator Entanglement

It was actually several years back when I realized just how extensive the diet of the bass can be. We have all seen pictures and heard of some fantastic dining accomplishments of bass, but unless we actually see him vary from a more common table fare first hand, the impression may not be that vivid.

An angling friend and myself had been listening to some surface commotion for some 20 minutes while trying to concentrate on some Lake Tohopekaliga bass fishing. Finally, we decided to investigate the activity taking place nearby in one of the boat lanes cutting through the heavy grass point that we were fishing.

I used the electric motor to get within netting distance of the commotion and found a largemouth of about five pounds with a 'jaw lock' on a chain pickerel, which was some three or four inches longer. The three pound 'jack', as many call him, was half-way into the mouth of the bass, but its whole head protruded through the gill plate of the largemouth.

Neither fish had an appetite any longer nor could they leave the table. They appeared to be at a complete standoff until I netted the fish, whereupon the jack slid on into the mouth of the bass and out through the gill cover. They swam off in different directions, a little worn because of their strenuous activity.

Just why a bass will attack a fish longer than himself is not clear and may never be. The aggressiveness of the largemouth is seldom rivaled in the freshwater world and they definitely can put away the groceries as their metabolism warrants it.

Yes, the largemouth bass will forage on about any kind of fish, bird, or animal. Anything he can get his jaws around, he'll put into his mouth.

The most dramatic picture that I have seen concerning the feeding habits of the largemouth bass is an oil painting by Edward J. Bierly, which was commissioned a few years

Bass that locate schools of forage to feed on, grow fat and happy. A primary prey of the largemouth in many southern waters is the shiner. Some very realistic lures resembling that forage are now on the market. An angler with the right bait can score high.

ago by Fred Arbogast Lures for their 50th anniversary. Release of the print depicting a huge Florida bass exploding in the bullrushes after a red-winged blackbird coincided with release of a new line of lures: the bird and mouse series.

As more lure manufacturers move into a wider range of natural bass forage, the angler's job of matching the currently preferred prey will be easier. If a lunker explodes under a bird perched on a limb and misses, then a lure that resembles that morsel tossed nearby, should tempt that bass to the stringer.

Predominant Forage

Knowing the predominant forage in the body of water will aid the angler in selecting the appropriate bait, whether it be live bait or artificial. Naturalized lures are the latest thing in fishing tackle and many companies are producing the attractive finishes on their lures.

Knowing the predominant forage in the body of water will aid in selecting the appropriate bait, whether it be live bait or artificial.

And why wouldn't a plug that has good action catch more fish with the realistic paint job than an older model? My feeling is that the natural look can't help but improve the success of the bait. Tackle sales of the naturalized lures are proving that adherence to the predator/forage relationship works. . .for the fishermen and the manufacturers.

Lures now come painted to resemble almost any widespread forage. Plugs are not only patterned after shad these days, but also imitate bluegill, crappie, baby bass, shiners, sunfish, rainbow trout, perch, frogs, catfish, crayfish, and other forage.

Some baits are extremely limited by the range of the forage they resemble, such as the rainbow trout. The range of this colorful forage in bass waters is limited to the larger, deep reservoirs in the midwest and east (Bull Shoals is one example) and some cooler lakes in higher elevations in the west. The rainbow is considered by many Californians to be the prime forage of the gigantic Florida-strain bass in San Diego lakes!

Forage Activity

The most important key to catching several good bass in any water is finding them in a feeding mood. Knowing the whereabouts of the major bass forage in specific waters is the beginning to successful angling. The activity of the forage can be correleated with the behavior of the bass and a relationship can be formulated. With an awareness of the forage and its environment and the response of their predator, the bass, the angler has a better chance to turn this knowledge into actual stringer weight.

As you take a look at the forage of the bass, try to develop an understanding or realization that to catch the most bass, the bait or lures should be, or closely resemble, the most prominent forage in the particular body of water that is being fished.

Knowing the whereabouts of the major bass forage in specific waters is the beginning to successful angling. The activity of the forage can be correlated with the behavior of the bass and a relationship can be formulated. With an awareness of the forage and its environment and the response of their predator, the bass, the angler should have a better chance to turn this knowledge into actual stringer weight.

We should form a basis for lure selection methodology from that premise. Match the artificial lure (or bait, for that matter) to the forage in all aspects. Not only consider action as most anglers have in the past, but also key the size and finish to the species of forage that inhabits the areas that are being fished.

As one specie of forage moves in to inhabit a particular area, such as crappie moving shallow to spawn, then concentrate angling in that location with a small crappie-painted plug. It makes better sense to rely on a more realistic lure than one that does not resemble any of the area's major inhabitants. Although waterfowlers have fooled their wary targets at times with crude decoys, most now realize that it takes an authentic replica to entice most ducks. Good bass anglers aren't far behind.

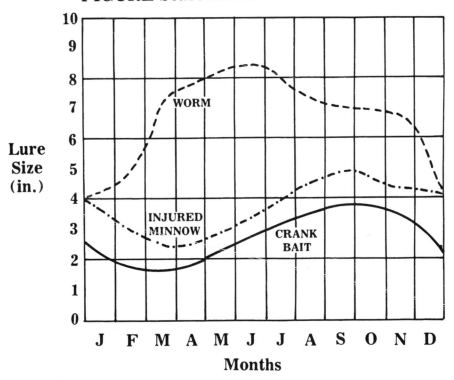

FIGURE-Seasonal Lure Size Variation

Seasonal lure size variation should be noted for maximum bass fishing success. As spring wanes and young of the year forage begins to grow, so should the size of the bait. The proper size live bait or lure replica will usually prove to be the most productive.

Trolling a deep running plug which resembles the threadfin shad through deep water harboring that forage, would probably take the most bass in such an area. Other lures which come closest to imitating the action and the look of a prevalent forage in a particular area should produce best in that place. Selecting an appropriate lure and following that forage fish is the easiest way to better bass fishing.

Forage-Filled Areas Where Bass Lurk

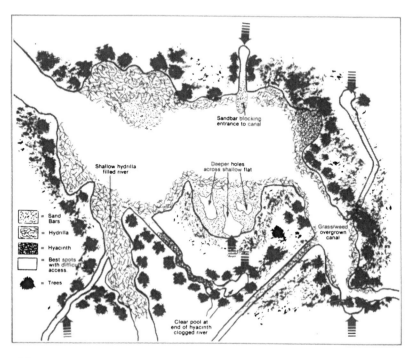

Shown is an example of some "hard-to-get-at places" that can really hold fish. Expansive shallow flats between areas of deeper water, "hidden" entrances, and cover-clogged areas are a few of the factors that cut down on fishing pressure.

Forage Behavior Influence

Knowing the whereabouts of forage will come from knowledge of their behavior as it is influenced by environmental factors, the food chain, geography, and time of year. Bass are opportunists! This predator, according to the fisheries biologists, can adapt to almost any kind of forage fish. Bass forage may vary from water to water, but the largemouth certainly knows where to find that which is available.

The predator-forage relationship between the bass and its food varies with the geography of the United States. Forage available in some locations is not found in others. Although the bass will eat anything readily available, it is more accustomed to feeding on forage that is abundant in its environment.

Matching the complexion and action of a lure to an available forage should be most productive for the serious angler. The maps in Part 2 of this book show the the approximate range of some of the more popular food of the largemouth bass. The information to compile the graphic illustrations was based on responses from fish and game agencies throughout the U.S.

The shaded areas within the dashed boundary indicate the approximate range of the forage. Alaska (not shown) does not have black bass, and while Hawaii contains bass, the prey differs greatly. The only common forage that is available on these islands is the shad and the Tilapia species.

BASS FEEDING BEHAVIOR
From The Bed To The Glance That Kills

THE BASS' NEVER-ENDING quest for food is his weakness. Their insatiable behavior is why anglers pursue the highly popular freshwater game fish. They grow fast and large, but their feeding activities make them susceptible to being victimized by an angler.

While a baby bass' mouth is developing during the first few hours after it emerges (tail first) from the egg, the yolk sac sustains it. Their eyes are 'bigger than their stomachs' from about their second or third day of life. By this time, their yolk sac has been absorbed and they are ready for the world. From then on, it's a continuous process of finding the forage to satisfy their basic growth needs.

Since smaller bass require less food for maintenance, a greater percentage of the forage can be utilized for growth. As their size increases, the food intake as a percentage of body weight decreases. They eat voraciously and continue to grow.

The size of prey consumed by the largemouth increases as the bass grows and a transition of food habits occurs. Baby bass feast on plant and animal microorganisms at first. Plankton and tiny crustaceans (zooplankton and water fleas) are the principal food for bass under two in-

Aquatic weeds and plants are home to the shiner and other members of the Minnow family. Bass know this and are attracted to such areas, where they wait in ambush position.

ches. They seem to feed endlessly. After four to six weeks, aquatic and terrestrial insects, especially nymph and larvae forms, then become an important ingredient in the bass' diet until they are four inches long. They can ingest an amazing amount of mosquito larvae at this time.

At about ten weeks, the diet of the fingerling bass consists heavily of tiny forage fish and other small, edible creatures such as crayfish and grass shrimp. They are soon feeding on anything they can get into their mouths including their smaller brothers. Within six months they have usually attained a length of six or seven inches and are not particular about what they dine on. Forage fish, frogs, and large crustaceans become an even more substantial part of food intake when they reach a pound or so, and as the bass grow older.

Inch for inch the freshwater bass is probably the most aggressive predator that swims. In fact, they'll try to eat about anything that they can get their mouth around, including their own young. This one had a one-pound largemouth in her stomach (and was not pregnant).

Fearsome Bass

When a bass reaches two to five pounds, he has matured into a feared predator. He gains the respect of all forage that is proportionately smaller. His diet will consist of ducklings, water snakes, field mice, baby alligators, birds, or any small air-breather that falls into the water. He is feared by those in the aquatic environment and should be by some on land.

The relative size of prey generally decreases with increasing size of bass, but I have seen some large bass tackle very big forage fish, such as an eight pounder that I found floating dead with a huge bream of about two pounds stuck in its mouth. Largemouths can supposedly swallow a slab-sided bluegill that is about one-third of its own length. Keeping this in mind when you go to the tackle box could pay 'big' dividends.

The feeding habits of the largemouth bass are influenced by degree of hunger, maturity and size of fish, sex of fish, spawning activities, water temperature, time of day (and of year), and the many forage factors. Influences as to type of forage include: size distribution, coloration, mobility, accessibility, abundance of primary forage and alternative food supplies, length of growing season, amount of cover, amount of fishing pressure, abundance of other predators, turbidity and productivity of the water, and armament such as spines or shells.

Digestive Influence

Digestive rates vary with several parameters which are keyed to the bass' metabolism. A bass won't wait until a stomach-full of food has been completely digested prior to feeding again. Many of us have caught bass that were spitting up food and yet struck at our baits.

The metabolism of the cold-blooded fish is effected by water temperatures. As the winter sets in, dropping temperatures into the forties, the rate of metabolism, and correspondingly, digestion is slowed. Food requirements are likewise reduced at lower temperatures. Feeding activity will be less influenced by the hunger factor since bass will feed as infrequently as once every two weeks in extremely cold water.

The digestive physiology of the bass limits the type of food it can utilize. Enzymes that break down protein and fat are present in its stomach and intestines. Those digestive enzymes required for breakdown of vegetation are not found in bass. A check of the stomach contents of any bass cleaned should reveal food in various stages of decomposition. It takes about 2 days for a bass to completely digest most forage fish during warm weather, and longer in cold temperatures.

Feeding Motivation

There are three types of feeding behavior which are commonly found in lake and stream bass. They are methodical inhalation, competitive inspiration, and reflex reaction. While the first two are hunger-driven, the latter is simply a response to the newly-found prey.

A solitary bass will sight his victim from either an ambush position or as he cruises in hunger. He will approach the prey with caution and open his huge mouth to inhale the food. The mouth opening will suck in whatever happens to be near it. The gills are flared simultaneously with the mouth's opening to discharge the adjacent water through the gill covers. The action is quick and the predator doesn't even have to be right on target.

The bass, upon recognizing a phony forage, can quickly reverse the action and 'blow' it out. The suction, while deadly to prey, is often hard to detect from the surface side of a fishing rig. Line stretch and rod-vibration transfer play a part in an angler's determining this happening on the end of his monofilament. Careful observation and sensitivity must be utilized to detect this type of strike action.

To entice a lunker bass to come up like thunder and murder a bait on the surface is a feat that will long be remembered. At times, bass may be 'on the feed', while other times it will be necessary to impulse fish into striking when they have no inclination to do so.

Eternal Competition

Bass are always competing with each other for available forage. When spawning production of the prey is poor, competition between the predators is even stiffer. Less food per acre means an unbalanced fishery and 'survival of the fittest' for the bass.

When competing with others in the area for the same food, they will charge the forage and quickly engulf it. When a bass is fooled by an angler's lure, quite often there will be competition for that bait. A similar one tossed near the action by a second angler will often bring a strike from a competing member of the bass school. Trailing bass are excited about losing the forage and highly motivated to attack the second lure.

Likewise when a surfacing fish pops a frog or bream, the angler who gets his lure to that spot quickly often connects with the feeding bass or one of his competitors. These fish have very little thought of safety when they are on a feeding binge. Even when a bass is full he may want to beat the competition to a newly introduced prey. He can't stand another beating him out of the food.

Bass normally school according to year class, but the size range may vary. A four-year old largemouth can weigh eight pounds or one, depending on how competitive it is. A school of fish spawned in a particular year will often stay together until the population dwindles substantially. The size of a bass school may vary from six fish to over 400 depending on the structure present and forage available. The weight of the bass may vary by 100 percent or so. Four pounders may co-exist with two pounders and be stiff competition.

Hunger Ritual

When feeding bass are motivated by hunger, they exhibit a unique behavior that includes preparatory movements. When forage fish notice the activity which includes a rocking motion of the bass' body and its gills flaring, they frantically scoot for cover in terror. Until the hunger urge and corresponding antics occur, the underwater world appears calm and serene.

On numerous occasions, underwater researchers and observers have viewed the ritual. Bass and other predators would swim among their forage, passing within inches of them. The potential food is unconcerned about predation and shows little caution. Shiners, bluegills, and other forage are not frightened by the presence of even huge bass. The obvious compatibility of predator and prey add to the tranquility and peacefulness of the aquatic scene.

Carl Malz, Managing Editor of "Fishing Facts" magazine describes the underwater ritual, as he observed it in Rainbow Springs, Florida.

"Suddenly, the entire mood and tempo of this peaceful scene began to change. Both the shad and the bluegill began to fidget nervously. Smaller baitfish darted restlessly from place to place. Other schools of roving baitfish deserted their open water positions in favor of stations located much closer to weed or brush type cover.

"While all this nervous activity was going on amongst the forage fish, one very large bass began to display a rhythmic flexing action of its jaws. The large predator flared its gills several times and this gesture was accompanied by a raising of the dorsal fin and an erratic flitting action of the eyeballs. The bass' body coloration changed slowly to vivid green. The black stripe running along the bass' lateral line turned even darker and far more distinguishable.

"From inside the sparse edge of scattered weeds, there emerged an entire school of very large bass, the largest maybe 9 or 10 pounds. Slowly they emerged in almost perfect unison. When they reached the outer edge of the weedline, they halted their progress momentarily, and this abrupt halt was then followed by the same yawning and flaring (of the gill cover) actions. Their eyeballs now seemed to click and dart back and forth, and their spiny dorsal fins were now raised.

"At that precise moment the bluegill, shad, and baitfish population went absolutely bananas. They scattered in every direction. The school of lunker bass charged from the weedline and tore into the bluegill and shad as though there were no tomorrow. If you can visualize a hungry

In relatively shallow lakes, bass can hold in the thicker vegetation all day. The bait fish beneath the hyacinths and pads and the top side creatures, such as frogs, snakes, birds and bugs, provide the bass with food. The thick cover generally provides the bass with low-light intensity, protection, and cooler water temperature.

pack of wolves intimidating its prey, then you've got a clear picture of what was happening down there.''

Such behavior usually lasts only minutes. The aggressive prowlers select their prey and quickly catch them. As suddenly as the mood has changed, the scene reverts back to calmness. The frenzy is over. The baitfish no longer dart into heavy vegetation. They emerge from hiding. The danger signals being transferred from the bass, are no longer. The prey is safe, for the time being.

Quick Reaction

The third type of feeding bahavior exhibited by bass is that of the reflex response. It is a reaction that is usually not inspired by hunger. Many of the strikes that anglers get are of this nature. The angler's lure splashing down near the fish may key the instantaneous response. The same behavior can be noted when a minnow is tossed into a large tank with bass. It is immediately hit by the nearest bass.

Often, the predators are full at the time of such behavior. They are triggered into the reflex action by a properly presented lure or bait. Speed of retrieve with an artificial bait to garner this response is dependent on water temperature, in part. Warmer weather brings on quicker actions and faster retrieves are responsible for better catches of bass.

Feeding bass can be "conned" into the response also. Those on the prowl looking for something to eat will pounce on a bait as it hits the water. Therefore, keeping a keen eye out for any sign of feeding will enable an angler to more often trigger a reflex strike.

Fill It Up

Feeding bass can be found in shallow or deep waters. Targets holding forage can be located easily in the shallows. Deeper waters must be searched with depth finders to discover areas that induce extensive feeding. Bass normally spread out over a shallow area as they hunt for food, but remain together on a particular spot while foraging in deeper depths.

Bass will fill up quickly when the prey is abundant, easily caught, and of substantial size. If forage is small or hard to catch, the bass will have to feed for longer periods. Food is burned quicker during such marathons and more is required. It is a continuous process, a closed cycle. Energy is burned rapidly while chasing smaller forage.

Canal entrances, small tributaries, and runoff areas that may have the floating plant trapped are great bass feeding areas. Good structure can lie beneath such places and the cover and food is just tremendous. These are natural places for feeding fish, and the hyacinth makes it even more productive.

Energy expended to fill the stomach is less as the forage base grows or better feeding conditions are discovered elsewhere. Bass require shorter feeding times. During cold water temperatures, bass feed less and less per dictation from their metabolism. Unless a bass finds warm water during extreme winter periods, its feeding urge will diminish substantially.

Forage Abstinence

Sex of the fish does play a part in feeding habits of the bass. Female bass are more active feeders than males which is good because they grow into lunkers, and that is what most anglers seek. Male bass are usually more susceptible to capture only during the spawning period when they are guarding the nest. Actually they seldom feed during this part of the spring.

While the males are building the nests, they will try to keep any invader away from the beds. They are very protective against any potential egg-eating predator, such as bluegills, salamanders, crayfish, and certain other minnow species. A lure crawled through a bed at this time will trigger the protective reaction, a non-feeding response.

Meanwhile the females are lying in nearby deep water showing no interest in feeding. Baitfish move freely among the ripe sows without apprehension. Female bass that do feed while on the bed often will take what appears to be injured forage. They won't expend much energy chasing anything. They'll simply suck in a bait gently and check out its edibility.

After spawning, the big females are physically spent. Their energy has been drained and forage is difficult to catch. Tempting baitfish can swim among the lethargic bass without fear, for a few weeks until they regain full strength. The easiest prey at this time is often their own spawn.

The young bass quickly learn that their own parents will eat them. Most large females are cannibalistic and smaller bass must stay constantly alert to survive. Some very large bass (four pounds) have been found in the throats and stomachs of trophy largemouth.

Depth Behavior

The presence of other predators has been found to influence the relationship between bass and their prey. In lakes where northern pike and walleye exist and compete with bass for young perch, some studies have shown the foraging of bass to be modified. The abundance of northerns, in particular, appears to influence the depth zones and type of structure that bass use, according to biologists with the Minnesota Department of Natural Resources.

Water level has a definite effect on the feeding habits of bass, and drawdowns, drought, floods, etc. can greatly influence the relationship. When water levels are up and into

When water levels are up and into dense aquatic vegetation, bass tend to feed heavily on crayfish which are usually abundant in the weedy shallows.

dense aquatic vegetation, bass tend to feed heavily on crayfish which are usually abundant in the weedy shallows. As the water recedes and vegetation declines, bass consumption of shad and bluegill usually increases while consumption of crayfish decreases. Utilization of the crayfish is relative to the amount of vegetation that a body of water contains.

Lake managers wishing to control the predator-prey relationship in their waters can usually do so through the technique of water-level fluctuation. Usually though, this byproduct occurs due to level changes for other reasons (natural, irrigation, runoffs, drawdowns, etc.). Regardless, knowing the relation of the existing water level to the normal 'pool level' can enable the angler to determine current feeding response of the bass.

King Of The Predators

The full-grown muskellunge may be "king" of the aquatic hill, but until they reach about 15 inches they are still fair game for other predator fish.

Inch for inch, the freshwater bass is probably the most aggressive predator that swims and muskies had better not get in the way! Actually more musky may end up in the stomachs of bass than vice versa.

The West Virginia Department of Natural Resources reports that one collection of spotted bass for stomach analysis revealed several fat and happy musky eaters. One spotted bass, only 11½ inches long, contained seven, six-inch long musky in his rather bloated stomach.

The sampling was taken the night after a stocking of the fingerling musky in Bluestone Reservoir. Three other spotted bass taken for stomach analysis which were found to contain seven muskies proved that this was no fluke.

PHYSICAL BASS
Senses Adaptable To All Conditions

THE MAGNIFICENT HUNTING MACHINE. That would be an appropriate description of the family of black bass. They are predators of the freshwater world with very few equals. Their senses are tuned to the underwater scene where the prey is easily distinguished.

Bass continually search for food. During hot weather, they may feed several times per day while the winter water temperatures substantially slow those requirements. The metabolism dictates the necessity of feeding, but a reflex response not related to hunger is often noted in the fish. Their ability to forage effectively is highly dependent upon their senses.

Hearing, sight, smell, touch and taste are all developed to accomplish predatory tasks. The senses can differentiate between multiple stimuli under a variety of conditions. They are adaptable to most water characteristics and enable bass to utilize the appropriate sense(s) for feeding.

In low-visability water, bass may hear the forage by the sounds it makes or by its vibrations which run through the watery medium. In clearer water, they will utilize a combination of hearing and sight to identify forage and to strike at it. Smell plays an important role in stimulating

the behavior under other conditions of water clarity. Once the bass has grabbed the prey, it uses the senses of taste and touch to authenticate the food value. At this time, the prey can be either swallowed or rejected as inedible.

Let's Get Physical

The bass is a brute. Many fish can outswim it at much higher speeds. Fish moving about the open waters of a lake (such as the striper) are generally designed for sustained speed. They can chase their prey almost indefinitely at very high speeds. The bass is different.

All species of bass are hunters who stalk their prey in and around cover. They are built for swift bursts and quick turns. Bass are highly mobile and no fish in freshwater can match their repertoire of maneuvers when trying to catch forage or escape a 'hook lock' on their jaw. Their movements and ability are like those of a basketball player versus that of a track runner. The bass can move up, down, sideways, and even backwards, requirements for effective foraging in its favorite environment.

Prey that inhabit dense cover often play hide and seek. Muscles of the bass are adept at winning this game. The large tail is capable of tremendous thrusts for a short distance. Bass that reach heavy weights are the most powerful of all. They have to be to become such effective foragers and to grow to huge proportions. Fish under constant current have also developed power and speed capabilities. River fish and those under tidal action are very strong.

The bass has a huge head and large mouth, alas, the name 'bigmouth' or largemouth. Even the smallmouth bass has a larger mouth than many predators. The jaw expanse precludes the need for pinpoint accuracy. It can inhale any prey within inches of its mouth.

The bass is a brute and like all hunters who stalk their prey in and around cover, it is built for swift bursts and quick turns. The bass has a huge head and large mouth, alas the name 'bigmouth' or largemouth. Even the smallmouth bass has a larger mouth than many predators.

Feeling Those Vibrations

The initial contact between predator and prey is through sound vibrations. Displacement pressures are transmitted by the forage as they move through the medium of water. The presence of a baitfish can be detected by the bass without use of its sight sense. The vibrations that are emitted can even be interpreted by the predator as to the approximate shape and size.

Sound in water travels four times faster than it does in air, at some 5,000 feet per second and the sound sensors of bass are atuned to their environment. Their range of hearing is much greater than ours. In cloudy water, bass depend on their ability to transmit the action of the object that they are tracking to the brain for interpretation.

In most fishing situations at night, or on waters of medium to low visibility, sound and vibration play a vital role in an angler's success. The acoustic abilities of all lures make or break their forage appeal. Lure manufacturers have worked for years trying to develop baits with the right action and corresponding acoustic emission to slay bass. Body shapes, spinner 'tuning', and built-in rattling chambers have been experimented with by the designers.

The solitary goal is to come up with the perfect bait that truly simulates forage and, in fact, stimulates the feeding behavior of bass. Lures must emit a similar sound vibration as that of the forage. The bass' lateral line must receive it and determine if it's edible. Thus, the lures action is critically important.

The Eyes Have It

Bass rely on their vision to enhance the perception of the forage transmitted by sound vibration. They have no eyelids and thus have to depend on depth and cover to regulate light intensity. Each eye is capable of viewing

Prey Fish - Most Minnows
Eyes on side of head

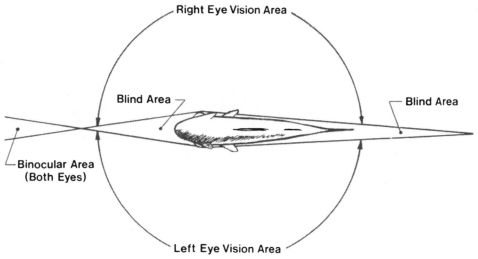

Prey fish (most minnows) have their eyes located laterally. This reduces binocular vision, but enables them to view in all directions to help protect them from attack.

Predatory Fish - Bass
Eyes in a forward position

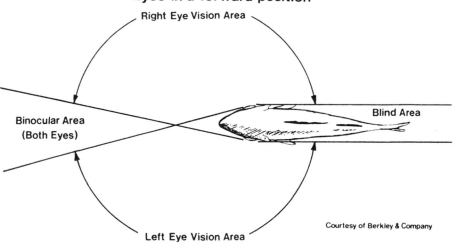

Courtesy of Berkley & Company

Predatory fish such as bass have a forward eye position. This increases binocular vision and enhances coordination and judgement when striking at prey.

Each eye of the bass is capable of viewing everything on its side of the body. Due to the protrusion of each eyeball, the bass can see over 180 degrees, as well as above the water's surface. Each eye is capable of tilting upward or downward in search of their forage or their predators (fishermen).

everything on its side of the body, Due to the slight protrusion of each eyeball, the bass can see over 180 degrees. Each eye is also capable of tilting upward or downward in search of their forage. Focusing is accomplished by moving their lenses in or out, as in humans. Electric impulses then transmit the information to the brain.

The color vision in the eyes of a bass is a great compromise in terms of light sensitivity and visual sharpness. Color is perceived by a network of cones with sight cells on the retina while the much smaller rods perceive black and white images. All night vision is colorless.

Creatures with primarily night vision have much more sensitive eyes than daylight viewers. The sight cells that are color cells are much bigger and much larger. They occupy a bigger area of the retina and therefore make vision less sensitive than black and white sight cells.

Sensitivity And Resolution

When a fish develops color vision, he is developing something that he will need. If he's not going to feed in high light, he loses a lot of his light sensitivity. Color vision is 100 thousand times less sensitive to light than the dark or rod vision (black and white vision).

Color vision is called photopic and black and white vision is called scotopic. The scotopic eye is much more sensitive and sees a much sharper image. Because the cell network is very much smaller and highly packed, it has a much higher resolution. The hawk has a complete black and white visual network on his retina and it can read a newspaper at 100 feet. Though the print is not any larger, he has the capability to see an image that sharp!

"Based on the disadvantages and advantages of color versus black and white vision," says Doug Hannon, "I would say that bass would not have adapted color vision unless they needed to see during daylight in order to feed. My catch records prove the fact that I've caught most of my fish in the high light times of day."

"The fish in my tank stay in the window when the sun shines in it and once they're used to people being around them, they're not hiding. They stay right up close to the surface," he says. "Even right through the middle of the day, as you approach the tank, you can see boils on the surface because they're hanging with their backs almost out of the water up in the sun."

Color Perception

Eyes of bass can detect small variations in color when the amount of light penetrating the water is high. Dominant colors beneath the surface are greens and blues. Waters that are murky or stained filter out colors, as do high surface winds. Under such conditions, the prey seems to take on colors which are close to the actual water color. Objects in brown waters appear as reddish-brown in color

Eyes of bass can detect small variations in color when the amount of light penetrating the water is high. Dominant colors beneath the surface are greens and blues. Waters that are murky or stained filter out colors, as do high surface winds.

while waters high in nutrients and vegetation primarily transmit green color.

A choppy surface will inhibit solar rays from penetrating the underwater environment. The rays are reflected and have little influence beneath the waves. At deeper depths and during periods of low light levels, colors are muted. The underwater world turns from warm, reddish-brown tints in the late afternoon to darker colors around sunset.

Dark lures look black in subdued light, but they cast a distinctive shadow when contrasted against the water's surface. Flash on lures used after dark often provide an additional visual stimulus. Bass eyesight under starlight is poor compared to other creatures that are stirring at this time, so the angler should select his bait accordingly.

In the depths, color shifts occur. At 25 to 30 feet red lures begin to take on a brown appearance and all colors, except the fluorescents, tend to lose their brightness. Fluorescent-colored baits retain their brightness much better than do

A choppy surface will inhibit solar rays from penetrating the underwater environment. At deeper depths and during periods of low light levels, colors are muted.

the nonfluorescent ones. Greens are among the last colors to disappear in the water medium, while red goes at 30 feet and orange fades away at 50.

Importance Of Eyesight

The value of good eyesight was never so apparent as in one of Doug Hannon's 'lab' specimens. It was the biggest bass in the tank, about 12-½ pounds when first introduced. The largemouth was not very fat and it didn't look healthy. The fish looked like a declining, old bass that evidently was just having a bad time during this period in its life.

As soon as he started feeding it, it became very responsive and gained weight rapidly. It didn't grow much in length, maybe an inch or 2, but it achieved tremendous weight. The fish grew to a length of 29 inches and a weight of about 17 pounds, before its decline.

"You see, it had just one eye and I knew it wouldn't make it in the world," explains Doug. "It just couldn't compete in the lake and live. It would never grow and it would just be a skinny bass until it died, so I kept it to see what I could do."

It survived in captivity a long time, until finally it began to lose the other eye. It started to get skinny again and ended up down at 13 or 14 pounds. "I knew that was the end," he says. "I had it for almost 3 years though, and it probably would have died that next year in nature. I was curious to see how long they'd live, and I'm sure that bass would still be alive today, if it wasn't for her eyes."

The food availability and climatic conditions have to be optimal for a lake to have the capacity to produce big bass. The ultimate lunker may spend the last years of its life primarily in heavy cover or in deeper water. Largemouth bass, as they grow to huge proportions, prefer subdued light to retard the fungus growth which eventually may contribute to their deaths.

Sunlight Is Vital

Bass are a sunfish, and one of their ways of keeping an advantage on the prey in their water environment is to keep their body temperature up. Because cold weather creatures' metabolisms work faster, their senses are keener if they are warmer. The colder they are, the more numb and slow they get. If the fish can keep a little bit warmer than his prey, he's got a little bit of an advantage.

"That's exactly why snakes come out and lie in the sun before they feed. It's to warm up their body temperature," says Doug. "There's a period of convalescence in the morning to heat up their system," he explains. "In the cold times of the year, they come out in the sun, and that's when snakes are dangerous. They'll be out sunning in the middle of the day, trying to get their body warm enough to feed effectively.

Small tributaries and run-offs harbor multitudes of bait fish. Bass are constantly in search of such places to dine well and their senses are totally attuned to the 'closer' environment.

"In the summer, when it's really hot, snakes are warm enough at night to feed. They're better concealed, so they feed then," adds Doug. "The worst time for snakes in the daylight is spring and fall, because they're out there pumping to kill, warming up to feed."

Many anglers only go after bass at night, but Doug is a daytime angler. He has caught most of his huge fish during sun-up times. Bass feed in the daylight and Doug has found compelling reasons to believe that they have always functioned (well) in the daylight.

Smell-Related Stimuli

The senses of a bass should be considered a total bodily function. Smell is an important part of the total physiology. Bass have two nostrils on each side of the snout. Sense of smell is accomplished by water passing in through the two forward nostrils, over a sensory padding of scenting cells, and back out the two rear nostrils. Since bass don't use their nose openings to breath air, they function entirely as a smell sensor or monitor of their environment.

Under certain conditions, smell is critical in locating prey. Dirty water creatures that remain fairly immobile can often be found only through the sense of smell. Not being a scavenger (bass want their food alive), their 'smeller' is not extremely sensitive. Still water environments such as lakes and reservoirs are difficult habitats in which to develop an overly acute sense.

Bass undoubtedly can distinguish the scent of certain forage at some distance. The body juices exuded by bait fish that are injured or punctured by hooks attract bass. This fact has led to the numerous scent products that are being marketed. Spraying them on plastic worms and other baits seems to work. Whether in fact they attract bass or simply mask the scent of the angler and any other foreign substances that may be offensive has been debated. Many authorities claim the former. Regardless, they work.

Mouth Senses

The sense of taste closely parallels that of smell in a bass and functions in conjunction with its sense of touch. Tastebuds are located on its tongue and upper lip. Though they are not well developed, the tastebuds can distinguish water impurities and level of salinity (or alkalinity).

A taste that has proved to be appealing to bass is that of salt. It is an important requirement for their body fluids and a definite part of their normal diet. Pork rind strips have been extremely effective on bass and Uncle Josh feels that the salt content in their baits probably has something to do with their great success.

The salt-impregnated Fishing Worm produced in Lakeland, Florida has been a big hit with area anglers who work the hundreds of nearby phosphate pits for largemouth bass. The bass hang onto the worm longer and allow a 'casual' hook set, according to manufacturer Mike Kennedy. They think it tastes like forage. While the salt additions to plastic lures may be an advantage, hard plugs are normally hit and quickly ejected if the angler doesn't set the hook instantly.

Bass baits are normally struck at through reactions from stimuli of the sight and hearing senses. The remainder of the five senses influence the ultimate bass decision of whether or not to swallow the prey. If it feels, tastes, and smells like forage, then the bass will judge it to be edible.

Overall, the sensory physiology of the bass is closely attuned to its environment. An angler who doesn't understand this is underestimating his quarry. Successful fishermen are normally quiet and keep a low profile. Shallow water bass are particularly easy to startle or spook by noisey anglers. While fish are in a feeding frenzy it may be difficult to shut them off with sound or visual contact, but under most circumstances, care in the approach and bait presentation must be used.

FORAGE PREFERENCES
Interaction Beyond "Thin Is In"

BASS HAVE A TREMENDOUS appetite, but studies have shown that they tend to have a preference for a particular forage type. They like a long, thin prey better than they do a short, fat one. They're basically efficiency oriented as is any predator, and that's just a natural course of evolution.

If they can catch something that's long, they can swallow something bigger than they can if it's short. In other words, a fish that has a 4-inch girth and is 8 inches long would obviously have more meat than a fish that is 4 inches long with a 4-inch girth.

"The bass tend to prefer the long thin forage," says big bass specialist, Doug Hannon. "I think that's why the injured minnow plugs are such successful lures. I can hold lures up to the window of my tank, different sized lures and different shapes, and watch the fish come to them. In a lot of cases, they'll come right up to the glass if they're interested and wait for it to move. If it is moved in a certain way, they'll hammer the glass after it."

"They'll come right to a thin, minnow-type lure just held in your hand," he says. "When you put the shorter lures, or fat lures up there, the bass will hold their position if they're interested. They'll wait there a while before slowly back-

"You can see preferences in feeding," says Doug Hannon. "Soft rayed, long, skinny baits (like shiners) are going to be taken a lot more readily than bluegills which are short, fat, and spiny." The Florida-based bass angler relies on his intimate knowledge of food availability and preference to determine the behavior of big fish and to successfully catch them.

ing away. When you replace it with a long lure, they come right back to you."

Doug has learned much about bass forage and the behavior of bass through studying "specimens" in his tank. Several years ago, he constructed a large, circular "study" tank in his backyard some twenty feet from Lake Keystone, near Tampa. The brick and cement structure is aerated and has glass "panels" around the perimeter for viewing bass behavior. He observes lunker bass foraging as though they are not in captivity.

Through personal observations, Doug has discovered various facts pertaining to the feeding motivation and preferences of bass over 10 pounds. His "lab" specimens are personally caught for introduction into the study facility. He has watched and studied them night and day for several years. His analysis of the results contribute important facts for potential lunker bass fishermen around the country and should be noted.

Soft Rays

"You can see preferences in feeding," he says. "Soft-rayed, long, skinny baits (like the shiners) are going to be taken a lot more readily than bluegills which are short, fat, and spiny."

"In my tank, I almost always have to trick fish into eating a bluegill. I'll get them going on shiners and then throw them a bluegill. They'll grab it. If they miss it, and they often miss the fish you throw, they won't go at it again. However, they'll give chase to a shiner and they'll chase it until they catch it or until it gets away."

"Bass will chase a shiner relentlessly but will make only one pass at a bluegill. Bass don't like them nearly as well. They prefer shiners," says Doug. "If you check stomach contents, however, you'll find the big fish eat mostly bluegills. This is one reason why lunker bass are beneficial to the resource. They go after the easiest thing to catch."

The 36-year old Florida-based bass angler relies on his intimate knowledge of food availability and preference to determine the behavior of big fish and to successfully catch them. With eleven bass over 14 pounds, his biggest (16 pounds) just 3 pounds shy of the state record, and hundreds over "10", his credentials have few equals.

"Shiners are a moss-fed fish," he says. "If they have really good protection in the form of a school and manage to get under the bass, they're gone. They're very fast and invisible. Bass have to stay right on them because that mirror reflection is hard to follow."

Bass will chase a shiner relentlessly, but will make only one pass at a bluegill. Bass don't like them near as well. They prefer shiners.

Silver Shadow

The silver or light colored lures are better because they imitate the soft-grey bait fish, according to Doug. The forage that has spines is usually colored and usually has bars and stripes on it, while the forage fish that's silver usually relies on large schools and open water for concealment.

Silver scatters light and is the ultimate camouflage because it mirrors everything around it. In the water medium, light is scattered, and if a silver bait fish can get below a predator, it just reflects the bottom and changes color as the bottom changes.

This is a mirror look, the silver defense mechanism required for open water type fish. These fish have to travel through the different color mediums, whereas the fish that stay in the weeds tend to adapt just to the color of the weeds and the bar stripe pattern.

The silver or light color lures are better because they imitate the soft-grey bait fish. The forage that has spines is usually colored and has bars and stripes on it.

"Weed-bound bait fish are generally more solitary," says Doug. "They have a spiny ray so that when they are bitten, they have a chance of getting spit out and a shot at burying themselves back in the weeds. They don't rely heavily on speed for the long term. They're usually short and fat, so they can move very quickly and just dive into the weeds. Then they just sit there and hope they're not found."

"The longer, fork-tail fish with the silver bodies move in schools in open water and are generally the preferred prey because the bass can get a mouthful of those things. He can swallow them any way, head first or tail first", says Doug. "When the bass finds long bait fish, it's easier for him to catch them."

Preference Study

His intensive study of lunker bass over the past 10 years has led to formulation of working theories and discovery of significant facts. The dimensions of Doug's aquarium observatory are about 16 feet round by 56 inches deep and it holds 7 thousand gallons of water. He built it in 1975 and has studied bass up to 17 pounds living in it. He normally keeps only 2 or 3 big fish because of the difficulty in feeding more than that.

"They eat most in the summer, every 2 or 3 days, so you have to feed them more then," says Doug. "A lot of bass can eat 5 or 6 bluegills and shiners at once, just as fast as you can feed him. Throw 16 or 18 of them in there and they'll have them all eaten. And that's probably enough to feed that bass for 10 days if in the wild."

"They eat a lot more in a tank and grow extremely fast," he says. "I can take a bass from 5 to 10 pounds in a year." Of course that is under almost ideal conditions. Other factors in the wild are present that influence feeding behavior.

Environmental Factors

Bass preference of forage varies with environmental factors, such as the amount and type of cover, the depth and clarity of water, the temperature, etc. The less mobile form of forage (for example, crayfish) are more easily taken by bass during periods of cool water temperature when all life forms move slowly. The size of crayfish consumed during these periods generally depends on the availability of the different sizes. Determining the most abundant size is the key to developing a strong, productive pattern.

The optimum size may be just less than the maximum body-depth of a forage that the bass can get into its mouth. This is approximately equal to the bass' mouth width. Since bass swallow a prey whole, the size of his mouth therefore limits the size of forage he is able to consume.

Easy Meals

Bass like an easy meal, one that is easy to catch and swallow. Sunfish are not as easy to capture as crayfish and

A lunker bass eats a lot of forage to sustain herself. She is somewhat particular about whether she dines on a crayfish, perch, crappie, or a natural-looking plug that may wobble by.

they grow quickly to a size too large for most bass to handle. Under such conditions, bass settle for whatever is available. Slow moving baits often entice them under these conditions. They come across to the predator as easy to catch.

A slowly crawled plastic worm will appear to be an easy meal, as will the injured minnow plugs. Bass seem to sense a crippled bait fish or snake and will attack it on sight. Bass seek forage that is alive, available and abundant, even to the exclusion of other types!

Bass' favorite forage, young shad, are often found crippled on or near the surface of a lake. They are not a hardy breed and are injured easily. They do achieve high popula-

The Primary Forage Seasons

Compiling the primary seasons for predation of forage by bass is difficult for a number of reasons. The many variables affecting the behavior of bass and their prey limit the accuracy of such an effort. Climate and geographic location, types of water, type and number of predator fish and forage, and habitat all influence the sometimes delicate relationship between bass and their food.

The chart presented here depicts the forage commonly available in many states throughout the country and their availability in the majority of states in which they appear. States on the extreme north or south end of their range may have to adjust the months accordingly. For example, the initial availability of frogs in Florida may occur 6 weeks or two months before what is shown in the chart. The state of Minnesota may have a later season for a certain forage than that shown in the chart and anglers there would need to "slide" the bar graph to the right a month or two.

The availability of each type of forage is encompassed by the total length of the bar beside the name. The month with the highest established feeding on a particular forage is shown by the dark portion of the bar. This is the month(s) that bass prefer to dine on that morsel.

The chart was developed through information supplied by state fish and game agencies throughout the country. Input from their biologists aided in establishing the primary season for each of the common forage available to bass.

Species of forage such as shrimp, snakes, crappie, small birds and ducklings, toads, and others are not a consistently significant portion of the "average" bass diet to warrant a place on the chart. Specific habitat and geographical areas of the U.S. can support a substantial predator-forage relationship with these species however. The season on this forage usually is not clearly defined, and trying to establish preference by the bass may be meaningless.

tions and maintain them, making them ideal for bass appetites. The plankton-feeding shad move deeper or into the heavy weedbeds at night and bass follow.

Small bullhead catfish have to be rated toward the top of a bass forage preference list. They are one of the primary

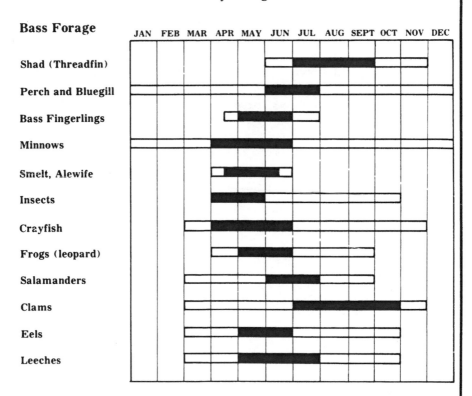

The Primary Forage Seasons

Bass Forage

	JAN	FEB	MAR	APR	MAY	JUN	JUL	AUG	SEPT	OCT	NOV	DEC
Shad (Threadfin)												
Perch and Bluegill												
Bass Fingerlings												
Minnows												
Smelt, Alewife												
Insects												
Crayfish												
Frogs (leopard)												
Salamanders												
Clams												
Eels												
Leeches												

entrees of largemouth and spotted bass in reservoirs and muddy rivers. The habits of the bottom-feeders track that of a scavenger. They are easy to catch and nutritious which draws the bass' interest.

Postspawn Preference

When big bass come off the beds, they particularly prefer very easy prey. They are physically spent and feed with some difficulty. Their foraging is relegated to the most easily caught prey while recuperating from the spawning tasks.

Smaller and slower lures are extremely effective for the postspawners. A slowly crawled plastic worm is perfect for catching these bass. Ideally, the bait should be inched along the bottom, barely moving. This target should attract the tired female.

POPULATION DYNAMICS
Managing The Food Chain

B EYOND PHYSICAL AND environmental parameters entering into the life span of bass, fishery management techniques play a significant part in their growth. In an effort to improve the bass fishery, the first step by most fisheries biologists is to study and analyze the water's population dynamics. Recommendations as to the best management of both the bass and its forage for a particular body of water, can then be formed.

Fish and game biologists usually try to promote bass growth and numbers to offset the effect of current harvest levels. A poor prey population correspondingly results in a poor predator base and often fish management activities are oriented toward manipulating the forage fish population. The number and size of the largemouth population is directly related to the number and size of the forage available.

It is increasingly apparent that management for adequate numbers and size of forage fishes is critical to bass management, according to biologists with the Missouri Department of Conservation. That state was mostly responsible for the extreme interest taken by other states in fishery management techniques.

Introduction of forage fish is, in fact, crucial to the game plan of many fish and game agencies throughout the

Fish and game biologists usually try to promote bass growth and numbers to offset the effect of current harvest levels. A poor prey population correspondingly results in a poor predator base and often fish management activities are oriented toward manipulating the forage fish population.

A fisherman cannot always be aware of the forage base, but he may be able to find out more about it by calling a department fisheries biologist in his area.

United States. Knowing when one species or age-group is non-existent or is not growing can provide the fisheries people with definite clues as to what needs to be done to improve the situation.

Recommendations as to the best management technique for a particular body of water can be formed from the population studies. For example, if a large bluegill population consisted of different aged fish all about the same size, a length limit might be established on bass which would provide more that were predator size.

The Perfect Forage

The south has been blessed with an abundance of bass forage and weather which is conducive to more variety of forage than in states to the north. With the availability of most species of forage year around, determining the best bass forage for possible management and stocking may be difficult.

Certainly the threadfin shad which range throughout most of the south, Florida's nominee, the river shiner, and even the saltwater-based shrimp have a claim to the title at certain times, under the right conditions. The Caledonian or 'bullhead' minnow, the crayfish, frogs, salamanders, and several fish species also comprise a relatively large portion of the bass diet at times. Bluegill, perch, crappie, sunfish, and even catfish are found in stomach analyses of bass. State fish and game and other independent agencies have been studying various species of forage for introduction into lakes with a lack of forage. These still incomplete studies will provide information not only on the best food (forage), but also on the best size forage for various sizes of bass.

Fishery biologists have determined that inadequate fish populations occur in waters which are lacking in one or more important characteristics necessary for a good forage fish. They either grow out of the forage size class too quickly, have too low a reproductive potential, are dependent upon stream flows for spawning, or cannot maintain their population in fluctuating reservoir environments faced with heavy bass predation.

Forage Evaluations

A study to evaluate potential forage introductions was conducted by the West Virginia Department of Natural Resources and Bureau of Sport Fisheries and Wildlife in the mid- 70's. Species considered were the threadfin shad, the alewife, the golden shiner, the fathead minnow, the trout-perch, and the brook silverside. In spite of its relatively ideal forage fish characteristics and apparent abundance, utilization of brook silversides by bass and other game fish was found to be less than expected.

The threadfin shad was found to be very susceptible to winter kill, although multiple spawnings did occur during the summer. Game fish utilization of the species has increased since their introduction in several West Virginia lakes, and throughout the south the threadfin transplant is currently the best management technique to rejuvenate an unproductive fishery.

Stocking The Threadfin

Threadfin shad have become a popular forage fish for stocking in many of the country's freshwater lakes. Fisheries divisions from several states such as California and Arizona have recently been supplementing their natural forage with the threadfin.

Introductions into new waters have proved to be very beneficial to the fishery. A careful study on Lake Martin by Alabama Fish and Game biologists of the effects on game fish populations from the threadfin introductions has proved that no degradation occurs to the fishery. Other studies in several states reached similar conclusions and the stocking programs are here to stay.

With the severe winters of 1977 and 1978, the mortality of shad populations in many of the more northern states has been great. The extra cold winters killed off virtually all of Oklahoma's threadfin, according to Oklahoma fisheries biologists.

In an effort to replenish the supply, the Department of Wildlife Conservation in Oklahoma is currently involved with the Texas Parks and Wildlife Department's fisheries biologists in a joint stocking program. Shad are being stocked into Lake Texoma, on the common state line, and into other lakes in the two states. This cooperative effort intends to re-establish the threadfin shad in many of their lakes that are now lacking in forage.

It is impractical to raise the threadfin in a hatchery for the stocking program, since it is much quicker and easier to simply capture them from a warm reservoir with an abundance of the fish. Then, transportation and handling is a simple process. Sources for procuring a brood stock of the threadfin for the stocking program are the tailrace areas below Toledo Bend Reservoir and Trinidad Lake.

Prolific Spawners

Once a breeding population has been transplanted into the reservoir, multiplication occurs at a fantastic rate, and soon an ample supply of forage exists for the various bass. Shad will spawn when less than a year old and they usually have two spawning peaks, one in the spring and another in the fall. They are also an open water spawner which makes their eggs and young less susceptible to many predators which frequent the shallow areas with heavy cover.

Dan Snow, President of Mexicana Bass Tours, who has been working with Dr. Roy Heidinger, fisheries biologist at Southern Illinois University, and Cuban biologists on a threadfin shad stocking program, has quipped, "Throw 20 shad in a lake and in a year, you'll have millions." According to Snow, Dr. Heidinger feels that it is possible for the threadfin to have up to seven spawns a year in the freshwater Cuban lakes. They desperately need some kind of forage in their lakes for the bass to feed on.

With studies being conducted in several states, the information generated on the threadfin shad introductions is amassing quickly. The future of the threadfin stocking programs appears bright, as does the future of the predator bass.

Seasonal Considerations

The seasonal extent of shad forage depends on the length of their spawning season. A lengthy season allows the prolific species to spawn several times each year. This provides almost year-round activity for the bass and makes shad-resembling lures highly productive under most conditions in waters containing that species. A short spawning season, however, will limit the yearling forage available for bass to just a couple of months immediately following the spawn.

The threadfin grows to five or six inches and remains good forage size most of its life. It is susceptible to cold waters, however, and as such, cannot survive in the northern half of the United States. The threadfin dies at 40 to 45 degree water temperature which lakes in many areas normally reach each winter.

The only way these forage fish can overwinter in many latitudes is in power plant lakes with heated discharge waters. In states such as Illinois which has stocked them in power plant lakes, the shad typically do not provide large numbers of forage until late summer and early fall.

The threadfin does have a short life span and it is most available for larger bass from July through the fall months in mid-south waters. Largemouth will school in the summer months in pursuit of the young-of-the-year shad which often form dense schools in reservoirs and lakes. Evidence of this predator-forage relationship can be extremely visible.

Other young forage fish which are important to the bass as they become available in the summer months, can be stocked to supplement the base. Bluegill, which normally spawn after the largemouth bass, can provide large numbers of small forage for fingerling bass which may be ready to change from an invertebrate to a fish diet. The availability of the young forage fish generally coincides with the most rapid bass growth of the season.

In many states, the bluegill is the prime forage for bass, but great care is normally taken with additional stockings of this prey. Bluegills compete with small bass for insects and other small organisms and tend to overpopulate waters quickly unless their harvest approximates that of the predator bass. That is not often the case, so bluegill overpopulation hits the lake's bass hard.

Too many bluegill result in a starving population of stunted growth. Bluegill fingerlings grow until they start competing with other fish where a logjam of panfish develops. Correspondingly, starving and stunted bass (which need to grow past 12 inches to thin out the bluegill) add to the lake's imbalance and poor health.

Minnows often play an important role as bass forage in the winter and early spring, then become less important as shad and bluegill become more available. Crappie, which spawn earlier than bass and whose populations are hard to control, provide some forage for the larger bass, but they are not a part of the fingerling bass intake. Stocking programs of crappie and smaller minnows are not considered feasible under normal circumstances.

Forage such as crappie, bluegill, and other panfish, plus the gizzard shad are all excellent prey while in the small to junior sizes, but they can outgrow the predator base quickly. Several other species of forage are too seasonal in the diet of the black bass for serious stocking consideration.

In late spring and into summer, the ways of nature often dictate that young of the year fish of any species may be open to predation by bass. When bass overgrow their food supply (and become hollow-bellied), they will eat the year's spawn unless harvested according to Mike Jennings, Georgia Chief of Fisheries. Additional management techniques are then required.

Predator Controls

Length limits and 'slot', or protected length range limits, are most often used to help balance a water's population when other parameters effect either the forage or the predators. To achieve this 'ideal' balance is the goal of most fisheries people and optimum conditions generally produce better quality bass fishing.

The thoughts on which kind of length limit restrictions to utilize to provide adequate protection for the bass, control of the prey, and maximum opportunity for anglers varies from state to state and even from lake to lake. Most state fish and game departments feel that either the minimum length limit or a 'slot' limit may be the answer to many specific fishery problems. Which 'cure' is currently used across the south depends on the particular water's characteristics and on the fishery biologist who is treating the problem.

When larger bass are overfished, due to lack of small bass, the lake population can become unbalanced. Forage such as the gizzard shad and panfish quickly grow too large for most bass to consume. Young bass that are present then have to compete with the forage for space and food. Life, for them is tough indeed. In such cases, a length limit to protect them and allow for increased predation on the forage (i.e., 14 inches versus 12) would be in order.

Regulating the catch can be achieved through implementation of a 'slot' limit which allows fishermen to take home a bass that is either above or below the range established. For example, 'slot' limit of 12 to 16 inches would allow anglers to take home the wall-hangers and, also allow smaller 10 or 11 inch fish to be taken. The slot limit leaves a healthy population of mid-size bass in the lake to keep the forage fish in check and allows the thinning out of a number of small bass.

With the advent of heated power plant lakes, the range of the Florida bass has been extended to most states in the South. Many of these southern waters now abound with the transplants which currently threaten (or soon will) most state largemouth records. A length limit on many southern waters has created trophy lakes and improved the angler's catch rate.

Fertility Influence

Population dynamics is concerned with the make-up and density of the fish available, in other words, determination of the percentage of the total that each species contributes, as well as the size range of each species. But a vital parameter in the population matrix is that of the water's fertility. The more nutrients (to a certain point) that a body of water contains, the larger forage base and bass population it will support. Naturally, fish life in a sewage pond with high nutrient level and low level of dissolved oxygen may be nil. Fertile lakes and streams are normally less clear in water visibility, but provide higher vegetation and forage levels.

The harvest that a body of water can withstand each year depends upon the ability of that water to produce a new crop and varies with nutrient levels, forage population, length of growing season, and other parameters. Overharvest occurs when the rate of take exceeds the fishery production.

The yield of a body of water that will replenish the normal standing crop may vary from 30 percent in the Northern states to over 100 percent in Florida. For example, if a lake has a fish population capacity of 100 pounds per acre and is capable of producing 50 percent of that amount annually, then overharvest will occur if fishing pressure results in a catch exceeding 50 pounds per acre. Naturally, for optimum conditions, the harvest rate will be similar to the water's production capability.

Fish and game biologists usually try to promote bass growth and numbers through better utilizing the available forage crop, and maintaining a better balance of the water's fishery to offset any negative effect of current harvest levels. A prime example of maintaining better balance is the results from introductions of the Florida bass. This strain of largemouth generally spawns about two weeks earlier than northern bass, according to several studies. The earlier spawn is a considerable advantage in bass reaching a greater size during the first summer of growth.

The harvest that a body of water can withstand each year depends upon the ability of that water to produce a new crop and varies with nutrient levels, forage population, length of growing season, and other parameters.

First Opportunity

Florida bass get an earlier shot at preferred spawning sites, fry have an earlier opportunity at available food supplies. They change to a 'higher-protein' fish diet earlier in the growing season. This competitive advantage results in higher survival rates of Florida bass fingerlings, and ultimately, greater bass populations.

The recent catches of huge bass in Texas as a result of Florida stockings, have honed largemouth fever to a sharp edge. Three times in 1981, the record was toppled, with a 15 pound 8 ounce specimen currently sitting on top of the heap. Lake Monticello, initially stocked in 1974 with Florida bass fingerlings, started producing impressive trophy bass in 1979. While most lakes in the area were producing 30 to 36 pounds of bass per acre, some coves in the 2,000 acre powerplant reservoir were yielding over 250 pounds of bass per acre, most of which were thought to be Florida's or the hybrid "superbass", a cross between the Florida bass and the northern strain.

John Alexander Jr. caught the No. 1 Texas bass as well as the second largest ever caught in the state. He caught the current record, a 15 pound, 8 ounce largemouth on an Arke jig and eel.

The largest taken from Monticello thus far, smashed a 37-year-old state record. On February 2, 1980, Jimmy Kimbell became the owner of the state's biggest (to that date) bass mark - 14 pounds 1½ ounces. When the crappie failed to respond to his minnow offerings, Kimbell switched to a crayfish-colored crankbait for bass and was more than amply awarded.

Since then, Texan John Alexander has led the record club. From the same general area on tiny Echo Lake, the current record (a "superbass") 15½ pounder, his previous state mark of 14 pounds 3½ ounces, two over 13 pounds, two over 12 pounds and four over eleven pounds were caught during the period from mid-December 1980 to mid-February 1981. While the lake has "cooled" since then, that is not too bad an accomplishment from a couple hundred yard stretch of a 175 acre lake!

Texas Parks and Wildlife biologist and Florida Bass Program leader, Alan Forshage, has been running studies to find out exactly of what the forage base consists. Crayfish and threadfin shad are very abundant in the lake, but the big bass Alexander caught that winter were full of baby bass. "They're eating each other," he told me.

As proved in Echo, Monticello and other Texas waters, the Florida bass and the "superbass" have been effective predators and are helping to reduce overpopulation of gizzard shad, sunfish, and even carp. Forshage opts that a 17-pound Texas bass could possibly come along at any time.

The Food Chain and pH Preference

Researchers have found that even the primary aquatic food chain is tied to pH! It begins with microscopic plant organisms called phyto-plankton that exist from the surface down as deep as sunlight penetrates. The photosynthesis that occurs in sunlight, raises water pH levels, often to above 9 in the summer.

Microscopic animal organisms, called zoo-plankton, live in colonies that range in size from a few feet to several acres, and they feed on phyto-plankton. While they migrate randomly on a horizontal plane, they generally follow a daily cycle on the vertical plane. The cycle begins in late evening, when they rise to feed on phyto-plankton, until sometime in the morning, when they begin their return to deeper water, until late evening. Zoo-plankton, however, can't tolerate pH higher than 8.5, which subjects the cycle to some variations.

The next step in the food chain involves shad and the other bait fish that feed on zoo-plankton. Shad feed mostly on zoo-plankton and follow the colonies through as much of their daily cycle as possible.

Shad are limited, however, because their preferred pH range is between 8.4 and 8.8. While shad can tolerate unfavorable pH better than most fish, because of pH buffering in their external body fluids, they can't follow the zoo-plankton everywhere.

Finally, bass feed on the shad and other bait fish that have fed on the zoo-plankton. This is just one food source that predator fish are involved with. Others would include crayfish, waterdogs, snakes, insects, etc. The pH preferences of various species are shown in the accompanying chart.

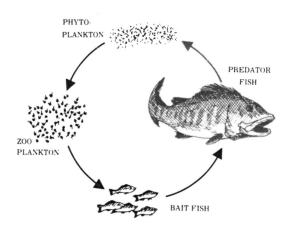

PHYTO-PLANKTON

PREDATOR FISH

ZOO PLANKTON

BAIT FISH

FOOD CHAIN

pH Preferences By Specie

Forage

Zoo-plankton	below 8.5
Shad	8.4 to 8.8
Shiners	7.9 to 8.4
Crayfish	7.3 to 7.8

Forage/Predator

Bluegill	7.7 to 7.9
Rock Bass	7.8 to 8.1
Crappie	7.2 to 7.4
Catfish	7.1 to 7.7

Predator

Largemouth Bass	7.5 to 7.9
Smallmouth Bass	7.9 to 8.2
Striped Bass	7.9 to 8.1
Northern/Musky	7.9 to 8.3
Walleye	7.2 to 7.8

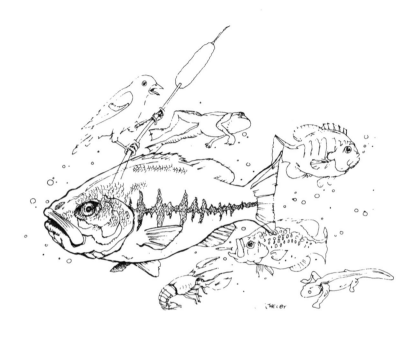

II.
UNDERSTANDING
BASS FORAGE

THE MANAGEABLE SHAD
Schooling Bass Love Threadfin

THREADFIN SHAD ARE a favorite morsel of the largemouth bass. As a baitfish, few rival the threadfin. They only grow to a few inches and are a more manageable shad than their cousin, the gizzard shad. Whereas the gizzard shad outgrows most of its predator fish in a year or two, the threadfin remains a more 'eatable' size for the duration of its life.

The threadfin shad thrive in huge schools which abound in most of the country's southern reservoirs and lakes. They are susceptible to the cold however, but can survive in deep water lakes and heated, power plant waters.

Their cold temperature sensitivity is important to the angler, because that fact helps him to locate the schools of shad, through the aid of either a water temperature meter or a chart recorder (depth finder). Just how to use those tools to find shad is important, and knowing the shad whereabouts can prove very beneficial to the angler. The depth finder or preferably the chart recorder, can be essential in a successful search for the favorite bass forage fish.

Elroy Krueger looked up from the chart recorder. "We'll have to wait for the shad to move to the surface before the

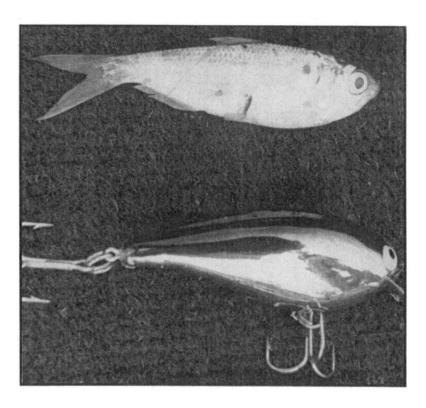

Both gizzard and threadfin shad spawn twice each year, usually in May and August, and they can be as populous as 10,000 per acre in some lakes. When there is an abundance of small shad, a lure of approximately the same size and appearance as shad should be effective.

bass will turn on," he explained. "Right now, they're on the bottom, in the channel and I can't even mark a bigger fish."

Krueger, a professional bass angler from San Antonio, Texas, and I were chasing bass on a small, power plant lake near that city. The late fall weather had been chilly for a straight week, with air temperatures plummeting to the low thirties each night.

Power plant waters are usually shad intensive. Heated effluent from generating stations keep water temperatures tolerable year around for both forage and bass alike. Lures that resemble shad are productive in the heated waters. Bigger fish frequent the deeper liars of such impoundments so the bottom scrapping baits are often best.

Cool Weather Effects

This cold weather had driven the shad deeper into the heated discharge water which ran through an old creek channel some 40 feet beneath the surface of the cooling reservoir. Vast schools of threadfin covered the 10 foot deep channel from one bank to the other, as indicated by the recorder. Thousands of the fish blackened the chart, just above the bottom contour line.

Normally, in weather like this, the shad will move off the bottom, toward the surface by mid-morning as the sun begins to warm the upper layers of water. Winter-kill of the shad is generally negligible in such power plant reservoirs with heated discharge water. The shad, however, is extremely dependent on this warm water source during the cooler months.

That morning was colder than most and a heavy fog insulated the surface water from the warm sun rays until late in the morning. Then, around 1:00 p.m., the shad schools began to move toward the surface, as Krueger had predicted. First, a few would come up, and then several would head toward the warming surface water.

Streaks showing the upward movement of the baitfish were burned into the chart paper. And soon, larger individual fish were showing up on the chart recorder, at a position about 15 feet below the newly formed shad schools near the lake's surface.

Gradually, the recorder found the majority of the shad to be near the surface and several bass began feeding at around 15 to 20 feet deep on strays making their way up to the school. Large schools of feeding bass never really formed before I had to leave, but we did manage to take several nice largemouth, the biggest around 3½ pounds. After pictures, all were released to once again chase the roaming schools of shad.

Reservoir Nomads

The shad, in their nomad ways, rove the channels and feed on plankton and insect larvae. They are usually concentrated within 5 feet of the lake's surface while feeding, since sunlight promotes the growth of the plankton. The water temperature has to be tolerable, of course, for them to be at the surface.

At times, huge schools of shad can be seen right on the surface, moving about in their feeding. On a calm lake, their presence can hardly go undetected. They usually avoid heavy cover, since bass may be waiting in ambush, but move randomly about.

The little, two-to-three inch threadfins will make small ripples on the surface as they cavort. When spooked, the school will seem to explode on the surface and disappear into the depths, usually to return a few yards away. This action is usually noticed by the sea gulls who love to feed on these fish. The gulls and other water birds will be swooping at the shad from above, which may just drive the

Shad are an open-water school fish. A cold front will normally put bass deeper and in more-open water. It is often possible to find a trophy fish near deep-settled schools of threadfin. Check it out with the depth recorder.

schools down to the depths of the bass.

Largemouth bass can usually be found 12 to 25 feet down, beneath the shad schools, and when they get the urge to feed, they simply move up. They will drive the shad into an excited frenzy as they try to escape the slashing bass. Dramatic surface disturbances often occur as the bass boil and swirl in the baitfish schools, knocking several shad into the air.

The bass will feed until they're full, then cough up some, and go for more. Maimed and crippled shad are left on the surface in the wake of the disaster, as the remainder of the school flees in panic. The wounded members of the shad tribe that escape the bass feeding mayhem will probably end up on a fatal flight with an awaiting sea gull.

Bird Spotting

The gull, like the bass, is never far away from the schools of shad. The gulls can spot the deeper shad schools easily from the air on a sunny day, and knowing where the gulls are can certainly help an angler to pinpoint the forage and the bass.

In the cooler months, from fall through the first part of spring, finding the area of the lake where the gulls are working or just resting is important. The resting gulls will usually be sitting over the schools of shad, waiting for bass to start feeding from below, thereby driving them up.

Bass will herd these schools of shad around the lake, periodically slashing at them and turning the surface water into foam. They'll attack the shad near submerged creek or river channel bends, near the edges of flooded timber stands, in boat lanes, through heavy vegetation or cover, and on underwater islands or "humps" on the lake's bottom. They will wait in nearby cover for these schools to wander by, and then pop them.

Shad will use the submerged creek channels and boat lanes to travel around the lake. They will try to stay away from their predators at the edge of the timber, but it is not always easy. They will travel the underwater paths which may also lead them through bridges, where they are again an easier target for the largemouth.

In such 'tight quarters', the shad are mighty uneasy and very spooky. And justly so, because once the bass have attacked one school, they'll simply retreat to their hideaway and wait for the next shad school to amble past. In more open water, however, the bass may simply fall back to a suspended position just below the feeding zone and wait for another school of shad to meander by.

All this surface action can occur year-round, depending on the lake. The bass schooling activity can happen in June and July on Lake Livingston and yet, just a hundred miles or so away, near San Antonio, Texas, the best months for schooling black bass are September and October.

I've seen bass schoolin' in August on Table Rock Lake in Missouri, in November on Santee Cooper in South Carolina, and in April on Blue Cypress Lake in central Florida. I've also caught bass feeding on surface schools of shad in January on one of the world's better bass lakes, Lake Guerrero in Mexico.

The threadfin shad ranges from Guatemala and Belize in Central America, north to Ohio and Pennsylvania and from Florida west, along the Gulf coast drainage to California. Oklahoma, Tennessee, Arizona and even Hawaii have populations of threadfin, so they're not only a southern forage fish.

Thermal Limitation

The range limiting factor is, of course, their vulnerability to winter-kill. Biologist have found that shad mortality starts at about 44°F in the southern states, while an acclimated shad population in a more northern lake may tolerate a slightly lower temperature.

Bass don't feel much like feeding at these temperatures, but when things warm up a bit, the threadfin forage will be needed badly. Oklahoma fish and game biologists have found that bass in Canton Reservoir prefer a diet of only shad in the winter. Stomach analyses have also revealed that bass can consume 3 or 4 percent of their body weight each day in shad.

Since shad are susceptible to cold water, this has the effect of concentrating the fish in warm waters during winter months, providing the largemouth with easy pickins', according to Texas Parks and Wildlife Department biologist Alan Wenger. "They'll move into the heated discharge waters of many of our power plant reservoirs," says Wenger. "And that will make feeding easier for the bass."

Although limited by water temperature, the threadfin can tolerate various salt contents. They are found in almost pure freshwater lakes, like Lake Livingston in Texas, to the other extreme of brackish tributaries along the Gulf coast, according to Wenger. They can survive in waters of 10 to 20 parts per thousand of salt content (the Gulf of Mexico is around 30).

The threadfin does have a short life however, which limits his growth. A two-year life span is normal for the fish and a maximum length of five inches is about tops for the northern-based threadfin. In the southern states, however, they may reach seven inches, but these 'giants' are very rare. The two or three incher is most common in the lakes that I've been on, regardless of how much plankton is available to feed on.

Wind and Current Influences

Shad will, of course, follow drifting plankton to feed, and bass won't be far behind, as the next step in the food chain. Plankton will drift toward shore with a steady wind, so the threadfin can be found in shallow waters at times.

The wind and wave action will also filter the sun's rays and allow the shad to feed nearer the surface than normal. Since the water clarity and light rays are determining factors in how deep the shad will be, wave action is just what the bass angler needs also.

The wave action will pile up the schools of shad on shallow points and bass simply move up from the deep after them. The mass of the shad schools is such that their location is highly dependent on wind conditions. High winds push them near (and sometimes onto) the shoreline. The lower light penetration brings them closer to the surface to feed, and game fish follow suit.

Plankton and minute organic matter drifts not only with the wind, but also with the current. Due to its light weight, the matter is normally found near the surface. Shad will move in such currents to feed and again, bass will follow the forage.

Current sweeps through bridges, along submerged creek channels and even in unexpected places on a lake. The current in heated discharge waters from power plants, thus

Knowing the size of the forage species at a given time of the year when they are most abundant greatly aids fishermen in lure or bait selection.

have an additional attraction for the threadfin,. . . food!

The shad will normally face into the current while feeding on the plankton, so an angler can determine a slight current by noting the direction of travel of the schools of shad. The current in some reservoirs fluctuates according to whether the turbines at the dam are running or not. Lake drawdowns and even navigational lock use can affect a current in some lakes, and this will often trigger bass into a feeding spree on the hapless shad.

Fishing The Schools

To the angler wishing to follow the forage and hopefully connect on some nice bass, several precautions should be taken once they are located. First of all, both the threadfin and the bass are allergic to noise. If either fish is actively feeding, excessive boat or motor noise will put them down deeper. Spooking one fish will generally eliminate the school from the angler's view. If bass are working the shad on top, the action could stop completely.

An angler in the schooling action should land each bass quickly, try not to lose any of the hooked fish, and keep the noise to a bare minimum. Any disturbance of the school will shut off its activity and the angler's.

At times, schooling activity can be great for the angler, but in many cases, the shad and bass will 'sound' before the angler reaches them. The latter is probably the rule rather than the exception for upper St. Johns River bass in north Florida. There is always schooling activity in the Palatka, Florida area, but seldom do the fishermen connect.

The bass will chase shad all over the river but, unless your lure hits near a breaking fish, forget about fried fillets. It takes too long to switch lures for schooling activity, so an angler needs to have handy a school bass rod rigged with a heavy shad-like lure. A tail spinner lure such as a "Little George" or the popular new "Whing Ding", is ideal for those 200 foot casts that may be required to hit a breaking fish.

The shad are usually corralled by bass in the river, near bends and at creek inlets. I've found that the most successful way to cash in on the action is to sit in the middle of the inlet and fish the drops, down into deep water. A shad imitation fished along the river bottom in deep water can lure some of the up-and-down bass to the stringer. The drops are always present where surface activity exists, since the bass would not be able to attack the shad schools so easily in open water.

An angler should match the lure size to the size of the shad that the bass are feeding on. To stimulate bass action, the lure should be worked slowly beneath the area where the surface activity has occurred. If you can't catch the eager school bass while they are slaughtering the defenseless shad on top, keep your patience and try them deep.

The occurrence of surface action may be more prominent in the summer months in many lakes, but some waters produce such activity during any month which may

Approximate Range Of The Threadfin Shad

Areas within the shaded boundary indicate the approximate range of the threadfin shad. A non-native species in the far west, the threadfin has been successfully introduced into Arizona and California waters and is now even thriving in Hawaii's fresh waters.

have negligible winds and warm surface water. An angler should always be alert for gull activity which could indicate that schools of shad are below and bass probably in evidence. Following on the trail of sea gulls and shad schools roving about the lake can be an exciting and rewarding pastime.

NATIVE SHINERS
Spawning Lunkers Hate Them

GOLDEN SHINERS ARE by far the most popular bait for largemouth bass fishing, and for a good reason. Bass love them and they also hate them. Lunker bass like to eat substantial forage most of the year, and the shiner fits the bill.

During bedding time, however, the bass frequently see the ever present shiner. Spawning movements stir bottom sediment, and when shiners pick up the scent, they move in to feast. Both the male and female bass will attempt to chase off the persistent and hungry minnows and will use whatever force is necessary to do so.

For this reason the shiner is a good choice for springtime trophy bass action. While they are an excellent year-round bait, shiners are considered to be a good choice during the cooler months also, since their metabolism closely tracks that of the bass. Although cold water bass are sluggish and slow, so is their forage during this time of the year.

The family of shiners is distributed throughout the states in lakes, sluggish rivers, and in small ponds. Most bodies of water have one or more varieties available for bass to feed on. Some of the more numerous kinds of shiners include the golden, common, spottail, and the emerald shiner.

Dead lining shiners over heavy bottom structure using conventional casting tackle is a top method for seven to 12 pound bass. An eight inch wild shiner hooked in the dorsal fin provides the action.

In the spring, the deep-bodied golden shiner exhibits a gold-color tint which is easily recognizable. They are the hardiest of the clan and can grow to 14 or 16 inches in length, making them a great trophy bass bait. Their range includes most of the eastern two-thirds of the U.S. and they can be found in waters of all acreage sizes.

The common shiners are broad-bodied and high-backed. They prefer moving water and can be found generally in the same states as the golden. The spottail shiner and emerald shiner are the 'weak sisters' of the common and golden shiners. They are least hardy of the family due to their oxygen and temperature requirements. The slender emerald shiner and the spottail, named for the black spot at the base of the tail, are among the prettiest of all minnows which makes them an easy target for marauding bass.

*The food source of the bass is very limited in the winter. Shiners are
the primary forage available, and they, like the predator, are sluggish.*

Spawn Interaction

In the late winter and spring, shiners frequent bass
spawning grounds. Although they are primary food fish,
shiners are mortal enemies of the female largemouth during the spawn. I first used shiners for bait many springs
ago in Florida. It was an interesting experience.

The bobber danced around on the surface and disappeared every once in a while during the shiner's first
minutes of freedom. Then he slowed to a methodical troll
over the area. My partner placed his shiner out in another
direction to better cover the area. The shiners were both
working well, as shown by the bobbers traveling in and out
and back and forth.

Although there was no evidence of any action from the
surrounding boats, my bobber disappeared within a few
minutes. I fed line out fast at first and then, as the bass

slowed to swallow her catch, I reeled fast until the line became taut, and set the hook. I kept heavy pressure on her as she headed through the sparce weeds, parallel to the boat.

Steady pressure finally turned her, and I was able to bring her out of the vegetation and toward the boat. The huge bass rolled into the net, and I leaned back into my chair momentarily exhausted. My partner held up 9½ pounds of 'beautiful' bass for me to admire.

Exuberant over my first bass of the day, I chose another likely-looking victim from the live box and tossed in the same general area. Within minutes, the bobber again disappeared for good, and the rod bowed with the heavy tension of another good fish. The heavy baitcasting tackle soon tired the twin of my first catch. Soon, the pair were finning easily on the gunwal-mounted stringer.

The water conditions that March day were nearly perfect for the day's catch which included two other largemouth over six pounds. Several other trophy bass that succumbed to the big shiner baits over the years have left fond memories in my mind.

Shiner Connection

Shiners inhabit densely weeded and protected waters during most of the year. They love small canals and sloughs just off of larger bodies of water and a good way to check for this kind of forage is to toss out a few bread crumbs. If any shiners are around, they'll soon be feeding on the bread.

Usually the best area to fish for bass is right where the bait is found to be the thickest. Shiners are there to feed on their forage, plankton. Many anglers will take a small hook and cane pole and catch their own bait.

In fact, most well-equipped fishing guides who regularly use large river shiners in Florida's big bass waters catch their own. they normally supply their parties with five or six dozen lively bait fish from the boat's bubbly live box. At $5 to $7 for a dozen of the finest, an average day's invest-

Most well-equipped fishing guides who regularly use large river shiners in Florida's big bass waters catch their own. There are two ways to catch your own bait. The most productive requires a good quality six foot radius cast net. The other, using a cane pole with small hook and bobber, should be the easiest way for a beginner to capture bait.

ment may deprive many anglers of another day's fishing with the very effective bait.

Two anglers can easily use 40 to 50 a day, and often, when the anglers are really into fishing during the summer, nine or ten dozen shiners may be needed to combat a higher hot weather fatality rate and fill a limit of largemouth bass. The anglers can either pay the price and stock up with the bait (if available) or catch their own. It's much cheaper to do the latter and even kind of fun.

There are two ways to catch your own bait. The most productive, via cast net, requires the most in equipment cost, about $100 to $150 for a good quality six to seven foot radius net. The other, using a cane pole with small hook and bobber, should be the easiest way for a beginner to come up with the bait.

Catching The Bait

FIGURE 1 - Hydrilla is common throughout many of the southern states and when it becomes dense, the holes or pockets may all look alike. The more productive ones to search for shiners or other bait fish are the ones near a current. Often, a flooded river bed will take a deep, wide bend which may create a perfect area to catch shiners in, just off of the slow moving water.

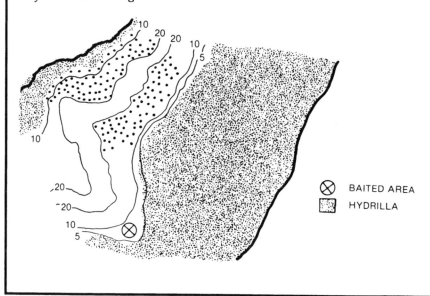

⊗ BAITED AREA

▨ HYDRILLA

Where To Look

Shiners can normally be found on the edge of moss or eel grass, close to moving water. They eat algae, so an area with plenty is important in finding the large schools. An algae film can be found on eel grass in some of the better areas.

They can be particularly hard to catch or lure near the range of a cast net in very clear water and fishing for them

FIGURE 2 - The banks of many rivers have multitudes of hydrilla plants which can hinder catching of shiners. Open areas, just outside of the main current, can provide shiner habitat in somewhat protected areas. For those using a cast net, the bottom should be clear of weeds and other debris. The areas should be baited and chummed prior to the attempted capture of bait for the best results.

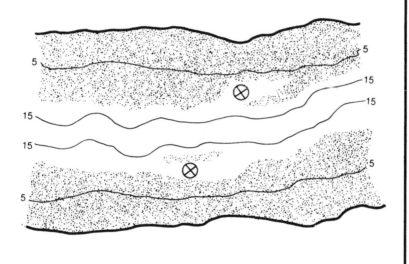

is definitely slower on a full moon than during other lunar phases. Early and late in the day are the most productive times to catch large shiners, but they can be easily caught over chummed and baited holes all day long.

The size of the first shiners caught will generally reveal the typical size to be expected from the school, but all specimens from the highly oxygenated water will require continuous aeration once on board.

Bait and Chum

The first step in the shiner catching process is to attract them to an area by baiting it. This can be done with one of a variety of good baits: soybean cake, hog or rabbit pellets, dog food, or anything with cereal in it. Even canned dog food with a couple of holes punched in the can to allow seepage will attract shiners to an area.

The cereal bait should be tossed into an area relatively free of weeds in about six feet of water for a cast net operation and ten to twelve feet deep for the cane pole fishing method. The best areas can be found by simply baiting about 12 areas and trying them all the next day to find the four to six that normally produce. The two or three best holes can then be rebaited for good results the following day.

Shiners can often be seen feeding on the surface in the pockets of heavy weed beds near the baited area but the bait procurer cannot normally go to them without scaring the baitfish away. However, it is fairly easy to bring them up to the boat over the bait. This is accomplished by chumming the area.

Although effective baiting requires 24 hours to attract a school of shiners to the area, chumming can produce in a few minutes. Quick oats, regular oatmeal, or bread crumbs, mixed with water and dumped up-current from the baited hole, should bring the shiners swimming.

Catching Them

The cane pole is the most common method of catching shiners and a bread ball the size of a BB is the preferred bait. The bread should be moist (fresh) in order to form a good ball and the hook size can vary from number 12 to 16. Guides normally use a long shank number 14 hook for ease of extraction from a hooked bait fish. This hook is less apt to injure and kill the shiner. A fish bleeding from the gills

A good guide boat will often have a specially built shiner tank which holds up to ten dozen lively baits. Great care is used in handling the shiner from chemically treating the live well for maximum survival to the hooking and casting of the fragile baitfish.

normally has little time to live.

The bait should fall to about four feet below the small bobber. When the bobber disappears, the cane pole should be lifted and the shiner swung aboard the boat and quickly deposited in an aerated live well. When the shiners are hitting well, a small white plastic worm instead of bread can be used satisfactorily.

Anglers with access to a cast net can round up several dozen shiners more quickly than they can with a cane pole. Four dozen of the bait fish can normally be netted in an hour or so over a baited area. The net is most effective over 'holes' totally devoid of vegetation since heavy weeds will interfere with the net's closing. It can be cast effectively over deeper waters (up to 10 feet) in dark, stained waters or on very cloudy days. Conversely clear waters and high, noon-bright sunlight require a quicker net opening and shallower areas to load the boat with bait.

Shiner Care

Shiner baits are very valuable and deserve great care. Aerators and a special granular chemical developed by big-bass specialists Doug Hannon and Tony Wheeler of Sanford, Florida's Jungle Labs are normally used by professionals to keep the shiners fresh and lively.

When Tony Wheeler, an avid bass angler, assumed management duties of the Jungle Laboratories Corporation in 1980, he had an idea for marketing a product aimed at anglers wishing to keep dozens of shiners alive in small live wells that are comon in most boats. Working with Hannon, Wheeler and his staff developed "Shiner Life" and "Bait Life". They also market "Catch and Release" which is more highly concentrated than the other two.

The ingredients contain a tranquilizer, a stimulator of protective slime production, and a bacteria killer. The chemical actually increases the oxygen in the water and prevents fungus growth. Bass caught can even be dunked in the bait well for a few minutes prior to their release. The treatment will speed up their recovery from parasite infection, handling stress, and other harmful problems.

Take Enough Bait

Taking care of the bait is an important ingredient in a successful bass trip, and so is having enough. I was on a Central Florida lake in January, a few years back, and did run out of the best size baits. Fortunately it was not so soon as to preclude my catching some nice fish.

It had been super cold during the month and the bass

Instead of simulating bass forage, which is what a lure does, bait is bass forage. It is authentic in appearance, in the movements it makes in the scent it gives off, and in the taste when a bass grabs it.

hadn't even thought about their spawning activities. They were still in relatively deep water and holding on a hyacinth line. My partner and I were fishing for Florida bass of the hawg variety. I chose the large shiners as our best bet to seduce a cold-water lunker in a limited amount of time.

Once on the lake, we moved quickly to a hyacinth jam and rigged our baits with 5-0 hooks through the lips of the 10-inch long shiners, small split shots to keep them down and away from the hyacinth roots and large cigar-shaped bobbers. We had waited only five minutes when my cork pulled the disappearing act as it 'popped' under.

I let the fish run for about eight or 10 seconds and set the hook. The stiff rod strained and the reel's drag moaned momentarily until I got the 'hawg' heading my way. My 20 pound-test line held and my partner adeptly handled the net and lifted the huge bass into the boat.

She weighed 12 pounds, 2 ounces that afternoon when she hit the scales, but it was the start of a great day for me. Although my partner couldn't seem to hook a hawg, I placed seven bass in the live well that totaled 32 pounds, naturally one of my better days on the water.

That bass was my largest ever (to date) and I owe it to a big native shiner. All seven of the fish were taken from the hyacinth line in seven to eight feet of water and all were caught on the shiners. The small three pounders were taken on the smaller five inch shiners that we were forced to use after our supply of large shiners ran out!

Yes, the best big bass bait in the southern United States is without a doubt the shiner. More bass lures have been painted to imitate shiners than any other forage. Before the naturalized lures were introduced, the shiner-color was on more plugs than even the shad, which has itself come on tremendously strong in the past few years.

Approximate Range Of The Shiner

The golden shiner is the most popular species of bait fish for largemouth bass fishing in the United States. It is distributed throughout most of this country, with the primary exception of the Rocky Mountain region. The shiner's range is dependent on waters with high fertility and to a lesser extent, upon water temperature.

Shiner minnows are a favorite forage of the largemouth year around. River shiners in Florida grow to 10 or 12 inches, but a norm for shiners in most states is three to four inches.

THE UNDERRATED CRAWFISH
The Dietary Staple Of Many Bass Species

WHEN CALIFORNIAN Ray Easley caught the second largest bass ever, a 21 pound, 3 ounce largemouth, from Ventura County's Lake Casitas on a live crayfish in 1980, the bassing world took notice. The small, lobster-like crustacea has regained prominence as a premier big bass bait. After Easley's catch, trophy bass seekers everywhere began requesting the crayfish at bait shops, while lure makers frantically honed their artificial impersonators.

Whether you call them crawdads, crawfish, or mud bugs, they're one and the same to the "bass" family including the largemouth, smallmouth, and spotted species. They love them. Louisianans do also for the same reason -good eatin'. While humans in 'Cajun Country' enjoy dining on the large crayfish, it is not the major part of their diet. For most bass species, it is.

The plentiful crayfish provides bass with a food source that is higher in protein and other nutrients than are forage fish. A bass generally does not have to spend a lot of energy catching a small crayfish scurrying backwards among the rocks and weeds. Their short bursts of speed, poor eyesight, and lack of stamina make the ugly creatures relatively easy for the bass to capture.

Another reason crayfish are so popular with bass, is their perennial availability in many lakes, ponds, and rivers throughout the deep southern states. Various sources list the number of crayfish species and subspecies in North America to be between 100 and 200. The numerous little crustaceans often comprise the major food source for smallmouth, spotted bass, and Suwannee bass and, even for the largemouth in certain environments and at specific times of the year.

The larger a bass grows, the higher its intake of the 10-legged creatures, relative to other forage. Samplings of adult bass stomach contents at various times of the year, reveal that in many waters, crayfish constitute some two-thirds of the diet. If you pay close attention to the stomach samplings of bass that you clean, you'll more than likely find two, three or possibly more skeletal or half-digested remains of the tempting crayfish.

Stomach Survey

A few years ago, during the first week of March, I was on a small southern lake which had an apparent over-abundance of crayfish. A week before a small fishing club contest, my fishing partner and I had taken some nice bass in 'pre-tournament practice. Another club member hadn't fared as well but did manage to catch a few nice sized largemouth for his supper.

My partner and I cleaned 4 bass each and examined their stomach contents during the operation. We found their bellies to be fully stuffed with small, one-inch long crayfish, six or eight per fish. During that week, prior to the Sataurday tournament, we searched tackle boxes and tackle stores, trying to come up with a good replica of the forage presently in favor. At the time, lure manufacturers had not jumped into the 'natural' craze and an exact replica was unavailable.

We rounded up a few lures to use, which, although being about twice as long as the actual food, enabled us to take third and fourth places in the contest. However, the other angler who has previewed the lake one week earlier had also surveyed the stomach contents of the bass that he had taken. Then he and his tournament partner actually spent all week building a mold and pouring dozens of almost perfect replicas of the forage. The coloring, size and shape of their creations allowed them to win the top two spots in that tournament!

Food Search

Crayfish grow much larger than the average one-inch long populace in that lake during that particular time, but after they reach five inches, their forage value to bass decreases substantially. They grow to such proportions over a four or five year life span. They are primarily nocturnal creatures, prefering low light levels for feeding and moving about. Crayfish do feed occasionally during daylight hours, but for the most part are very cautious in their movements between rocks, under leaves, and through ledge crevices and weedbeds along the lake bottom or river bed.

The fresh water crustaceans generally hide under logs, rocks, weeds, or other protective cover. Their diet, found around the bottom habitat, consists of both vegetable and

Crayfish are readily taken by bass in the late spring and early summer as they become available and vulnerable to the predators. At this time, a crayfish 'clone' such as this Bagley bait can be dynamite.

animal matter. They are scavengers, living on whatever they can pick up. Eel grass, algae, plankton, tiny snails make up a part of their intake, as do small minnows and decomposing animal life. They are also cannibalistic, preying on smaller members of their own species. On the whole, they are not sufficiently agile to capture a great deal of food alive.

When searching for food, crayfish may crawl in any direction, but mainly go forward. When accosted in open water by a bass or other predator, the crayfish can propel itself by flapping its powerful tail fan. The "bug" will initially try to defend itself with its pincer claws in a standoff and will resort to the backward ejection only if the waving claws are considered a bluff. The large claws are more normally used to tear its food into edible portions.

The claws are also used to help the crayfish burrow into the mud, to survive periods of drought or the winter season. When the water temperature drops into the fifties, crayfish become very inactive and soon go about their winter hibernation ritual - burrowing deep into the bottoms of streams and lakes. At this time, they become inaccessible as a prey. When temperatures rise into the fifties, the crustaceans pop out into the predator-prey cycle once again.

The Spawn

As waters warm to the sixties, the "bugs" regain full activity and begin their love-making chores. The males exude a viscous fluid containing sperm onto the underside of the female at a point near its midsection. The fluid hardens into a "tar-like" substance and remains there until the female lays her eggs which become attached to the paddles under the tail. The eggs are fertilized when the female scratches the dark sperm sac with the tips of her legs.

Hatching takes place in a few weeks and the larvae are nearly transparent and are spider-like in appearance. The newly hatched crustaceans are capable of very little movement at first, but after going through a number of molts they eventually gain coloration and the full mobility of a bottom dwelling animal. Crayfish will normally mate once or twice a year, having several hundred offspring. While small, the miniature lobster replicas are very succeptible to predation, diseases, and casualty due to variations in the elements. Those that survive have their Mr. MaGoo eyesight to contend with.

Coloration of the survivors generally depends upon the water chemistry and, in part, on what their primary diet consists of. A tinge of orange is often exhibited along their bellies and the lower parts of their pincers. The remainder of their bodies could be brown, green, tan, or even black as night, such as one huge, six-inch specimen that I seined from a roadside ditch several years ago.

As a crustacean, regeneration powers are inherited. If legs or pincers are removed by a predator, the crayfish will grow new ones, which may be, at the following molt, about two-thirds of the size of the lost appendages. With pincers and most legs removed, the crayfish is still remarkably adept at feeding and living until it has regenerated the new equipment.

Confrontations

Without the pincers, crayfish are unable to fend off attackers. Bass which spot a crayfish moving over bottom debris will stalk the prey. The confrontation will usually result in the "bug" snapping its claws at the predator in as menacing a fashion as possible. The standoff is normally temporary and when the cautious bass musters the inclination to strike, he'll do so quickly.

If the crayfish stands its ground rather than fleeing, it will more than likely, lose a pincer. Normally, the bass quickly tries to disarm the prey by removing a raised claw. He'll seize the crayfish by the pincer and shake it violently until the claw breaks off. The bass will often eject the claw and try to remove the second one the same way. Once declawed, the prey is eaten quickly.

This ritual is generally followed by bass in the one to three pound range, although at times, small bass will gobble up a "bug", claws and all. The small, two-inch variety and soft-shelled crayfish are most succeptible to being engulfed fully armed by a bass. Lunker bass will literally suck in a hapless crayfish from a foot away. He'll waste little time or energy messing with the removal of armament. My experience in stomach-sampling over the years, tends to bear this out - skeletal remains in larger bass, more often than not, included at least one pincer, while small bass stomach contents usually had no such appendage when stuffed with a three-inch or longer crayfish.

Growth Molting

Not only are the claws and legs regenerative, but so is the crayfish's armor-like outer shell. As it grows, the shell must be shed and re-grown continually. This shedding of the skeleton, or molting, occurs more often in the young, as they grow into adults. The crayfish simply outgrows its shell, splits it open and crawls out. This happens from a couple of times, up to a dozen or so each year, depending on the water temperature, its chemistry, and again, the age of the "bug".

The entire molting process may take a couple of days, but a lot happens. As the hard encasement weakens in preparation for the peeling and growth of a new external skeleton, the crayfish emits a hormone scent which attracts predators at this extremely vulnerable stage. The "bug" has an extreme requirement for calcium at this time, and actually absorbs it into the body organs from the hard shell being discarded. This, in itself, weakens the old coat, but the crayfish needs that calcium for formation of a larger garment. Cannibalization occurs more frequently during the molting stage, as the crayfish attempts to satisfy its requirement for additional calcium.

The hard shell of the crayfish prior to peeling will usually turn dark brown or black and the decaying coat often ex-

Smallmouth bass prefer shoals in rapid waters, while the largemouth will seek out quieter sites. Both love crayfish which compose about 50 to 80 percent of their diet. I prefer to float river systems during high water periods due to the bottom-scraping shoals. The rainy season is a good bet for adequate water, and this is probably the best time of year to catch some crayfish-feeding lunkers.

hibits a rough 'finish' from parasite attachments. Once the old shell is shed, the soft-shelled crayfish is totally helpless and vulnerable to all predators. The texture of the new duds is soft and jelly-like, and its external coloration is pale and transparent.

Soft-shelled "bugs" are definitely a delicacy for bass. For the live bait fishermen, they are the choice by a landslide. The excellent bait is often difficult to find, but with it comes a 'big bass guarantee'. The first time that I discovered a "softy" in my 12-foot seine about 25 years ago, I thought it was a decomposing crustacean. Fortunately, I didn't toss it back - it caught a two pound bass for me!

Crayfish can be gently squeezed to determine whether or not they are molting. If the shell cracks easily, the "bug" can be peeled and used for bait immediately. Or it can be put in a bait box and allowed to shed the coat naturally, which would occur within a few days. In either case, the result will be a great bait for bass.

As the soft shell begins absorbing calcium from the internal organs (primarily through the blood), the new skeleton hardens. The shell toughens as the crayfish gains strength to again be mobile and able to defend itself against some predataors. At this stage the crayfish is an exceptional bait, able to fight off the small predators yet truly a morsel for the bass.

The molting process is concluded when the "overcoat" hardens to a slick, tough texture. He is fully capable of defense and offense with his armament. As a bait, the hard-shell is the poorest. Crayfish in various stages of molting should receive priority in bait selection. They are more abundant in hard shells, however, and these should be used rather than discarded.

My father introduced me to fishing live crayfish for bass in the late fifties on an Ozark lake. He bought a couple dozen "crawdads" and anchored on a brushy, rock-strewn point one evening. The tailhooked bait occasionally found its way into rock crevices, but our stringer, after fishing the last two hours of daylight, was impressive. A half dozen smallmouth bass and one largemouth each pushing three pounds made our trip to that lake memorable.

Ultimate Crayfish Lovers

Crayfish like rocky areas on lakes and streams and so do bass, particularly smallmouth and spotted bass. In fact, these two major species of bass may be the ultimate crayfish lovers. Their distribution is in most major river systems and in many hill country reservoirs throughout the states. They prefer stream-like areas such as steep, sloping banks and points with rock and gravel substrate where forage is abundant. Rip-rap along dams and road embankments often attracts smallmouth and spotted bass because small currents wash hapless crayfish their way.

There are actually several separate species of spotted bass in the United States, with the Kentucky being the most widespread. The smaller Guadalupe spotted bass, a species unique to Texas, and found only in the Guadalupe, Colorado, and San Antonio Rivers and their tributaries, loves the crustaceans too.

Habitat preference is a key in knowing where to look for spotted bass. The stream heritage is evident in their feeding habits. They prefer insects, mullusks, and crustaceans, and one of the most irresistible baits to use is obviously the crayfish.

Live crayfish baits are often good in stream-type areas due to the alkaline level of the water. Rocky areas high in lime content, have a higher pH value (more alkaline) which is often conducive to more frequent molting. This means that soft-shelled crayfish are more numerous and there is a good chance that the bass will feed more heavily on such forage. This prime forage abundance will dictate specific feeding preferences of bass.

Check the area adjacent to the water for hardwood trees (cypress, oak, aspen, magnolia) versus pine. The former denote a higher pH. Exceptionally clear water year-round is indicative of acidic water (low pH). Crayfish prefer a pH of 7.3 to 7.8, while largemouth and smallmouth bass prefer a range of 7.5 to 7.9 and 7.9 to 8.2, respectively.

Limestone Bass Food

Limestone outcroppings, such as those found in northern Florida and south Georgia, are evidence of a water with high alkaline content. One such area, that of the Suwannee River watershed, has numerous swift, rocky stretches which are full of crayfish. The river and its tributaries also contain the crustacean-loving Suwannee bass, a rare species endemic to that watershed.

The short, chunky fish which closely resembles a smallmouth bass, seldom ever exceeds 12 inches. It has a bluish lower jaw and brown sides with diamond-shaped blotches. The Suwannee bass hang out in shoal areas where exposed irregular limestone or limestone rubble are prominent. They feed in the areas where eddies meet the fast waters or where underwater drop offs "buffer" the current.

Stomach analyses have shown that crayfish compose about 80 percent of their diet. Knowing this dining characteristic, I was able to recently establish a line-class world record for the little bass specie with a crayfish-painted crank bait -- the Mann Crawdad. A friend, accompanying me also established a line-class record with the World Freshwater Fishing Hall of Fame (Hayward, Wisconsin). Our plugs were cast to the crayfish-laden shoals and worked back along the rocky bottom to entice the action.

The calcareous spring water introduced through the limestone substrate is extremely attractive to crayfish. The geological and chemical features of water quality, the environmental stability and narrow water temperature range make these waters prime for lovers of crayfish and for anglers in search of those lovers. Float trips down such waters in the south on a summer day can result in beautiful catches of both smallmouth bass (Suwannee when available) plus largemouth. On the beautiful Suwannee River, you'll catch 3 or 4 times as many largemouth bass as you will other bass species. You will on other rivers too, where spotted bass, redeye, and smallmouth are numerous.

Live crayfish on such waters, or on reservoirs are usually productive if fished properly in the right places. Find the right places by looking for them. Spend a few minutes cruising shallow water looking for the crustaceans scurrying about as they evade you and your water craft. If crayfish presence is noted, then the waters will be ideally suited for bass also. Again, low light levels and springtime are prime forage activity times for the crayfish and, correspondingly, for the use of live crawdads or the imitiation plugs.

Baiting Up

Crayfish can be used as effective bass bait through several hooking arrangements. Super glue is often used to affix the crustacean to a 3/0 or 4/0 Tru-Turn hook. Put a drop and the hook on the crayfish shell and wait a minute or so for live bait with full mobility. Likewise, two small rubberbands can be used to secure the bait. One band goes around its midsection, while the other is fitted over the pincers and head to hold the hook tightly, which is threaded under the bands. The point of the hook is positioned to lie against the crayfish's side. The rotating hook will ensure a hook-up when it comes in contact with a bass mouth.

The crayfish can also be impaled on the hook. A popular method is to run the short shank, 4/0 weedless hook through the last joint of the tail (with hook point up). Hooking it through the center or upper part of the body can damage internal organs, causing quick death. When hooked "midtail", the natural movement of the crayfish is inhibited. Since crayfish travel quickly backward, the hooking should be "legit". The bait can crawl forward on the bottom and be pulled free of any temporary hangups it finds.

Fish the crayfish on the bottom with as small a weight as possible. A single split shot about a foot from the bait should suffice, with even bait casting tackle, and not limit the crayfish's movement. A small slip-sinker rigged behind a swivel and 12-inch leader is also a popular rig for areas with current. The rig should afford maximum mobility for the bait and a natural appearance in the presentation.

Often the crayfish will crawl under logs or rocks for concealment and hang on to the obstruction with their pincers. For this reason, I prefer to disarm them by crushing the pincers and leaving them on the bait. The claws become ineffective in warding off bass or hanging on to tangles. They'll still wave the pincers, but a bass won't be held off from his meal for as long. This is particularly important on the hardshell variety.

Hard-shells with full armament are especially adept at getting hung up when fished on the bottom terrain. To make them even more productive, try stripping off several segments of the outer tail skin at the front, leaving the rear two sections for maintaining hook implantment.

When still-fishing a sloping bank with cover, tug on the crayfish every 20 to 30 seconds to keep it out of mischief. A slow, constant retrieve will also work, but remember, the slower, the better with this live bait. When a bass inhales the crayfish, go ahead and set the hook; most baits are bite-sized and will totally fit inside a bass mouth.

The live crayfish method of catching bass has been around a long time, but people like Ray Easley are going to keep it fresh in people's minds. Anglers got away from the technique, but it is back, particularly for the trophy-size fish.

Catching And Storing Crayfish

All excellent bass baits are not easy to come by at the local bait shop. For example, the crayfish is found at bait dealers in some areas while in many other areas, they are extremely scarce. Those that do not carry the fine bait, claim a lack of demand justifies their reluctance to supply the crayfish.

For those that have to or want to catch their own (its cheaper that way), the crayfish is relatively easy to capture. There are a variety of methods that work and probably the easiest is to seine them. Roadside ditches, small sloughs, muddy ponds, low lying areas after a rain, or any shallow, confined water hole are excellent places to pull a 14-foot seine. The net should be kept firmly on the bottom as two people slowly move it through, at times, heavy weed beds, stick ups, rocks, and mud in waters less than 3 feet in depth.

Often two or three dozen crayfish can be captured with a 'pull' of only 20-feet or so. In a stream, place the seine across the current and then stir up the rocks and vegetation downstream with a garden rake, a hoe, or by hand. The crayfish flushed from hiding will flush upstream and end up in the net. If moving the seine in flowing water, work downstream with the net for maximum take. The rake can also be used to drag weeds onto the bank to check for concealed crayfish.

Rocks in clear water can be turned over by hand in search of crayfish burrows, and confused inhabitants can be grabbed or dip-netted. At night, a spotlight in the shallows can reveal big crayfish, active all over the bottom. They can easily be caught by fishing for them after dark, or in muddy water during daylight hours. Hook a piece of liver, bacon, lunch meat, fish meat, or any meat scrap onto a string and lower it into a cluvert or other dark, muddy water hole. Pull the bait out slowly and you should have a few hanging onto it. Grab them quickly when they are flipped onto shore.

The final way to catch a bunch of the critters is to use baited crayfish traps, wire boxes with a conical hole in one end and bait inside. Leave it in a shallow pond or rock-strewn flat overnight with bait of fish scraps, rotten vegetables, etc., as the attraction. Check

A styrofoam cooler with an inch of water in the bottom and weeds will keep a dozen or so crayfish lively for days. Grass shrimp will stay fat and ready for the hook also.

regulations for restrictions on the trap in local waters.

Once you have got a mess of crayfish, storing them is easy. A styrofoam cooler with an inch of water in the bottom and plenty of peatmoss or weeds will keep them happy. Use ice to keep them cool, or refrigerate them overnight for the best-conditioned bait. If pincers are large and space is small, disarm them because they'll want to fight each other. Keep the soft-shells separate from the rest and don't drown the crayfish by keeping them in too much water.

Even if bait shops in your area carry the bass-tempting morsel, catching your own in the water you're going to fish may still be best. You'll discover color-schemes for plug consideration when you run out of the live stuff and you may come across more soft-shelled specimens.

SPORT FISH AND
OTHER FINGERLINGS
Panfish, Bullheads, Tilapia, Mullet
And Baby Bass As The Food

WHILE SHAD AND SHINERS are important ingredients in the diet of many bass throughout the country, many other small fish end up on their menu. They feast on fingerlings that are abundant in their particular waters. Bass are opportunists that recognize their forage and develop preferences.

Bass feed on fingerlings of rough fish, catfish and other game fish that may grow to a large size fairly quickly, taking them out of the forage class. Carp, buffalo, drum, and bullhead catfish are part of the intake of muddy water bass.

Pickerel, walleye, and even white bass are largemouth forage while in a miniature size. Rainbow trout are a definite forage asset to the Florida bass fishery found in San Diego lakes where huge bass are fattening up on their neighbors and record size fish have grown quickly.

Nationwide, though, the favorite forage fish of the largemouth is members of his own family, the sunfish. Among the several species within that family, the bluegill ends up in the mouth of a bass more often than any other.

Bluegill and other sunfish, such as the Redbreast and Redear have been used for bait in many waters, but some states prohibit their use as bait. It is wise to check state regulations prior to using the 'real thing'.

Ever-Present Bluegill

Most anglers who have spent a considerable amount of time on the water have seen examples of the bass' voracious appetite for large bluegills. Literally thousands of bass have met their fates with an oversized forage fish stuck in their mouths. The broad-sided bluegill has sharp and spiny dorsal fins. If the predator bass takes it head first, and if his mouth is too small, seldom will the sunfish be able to 'back out'. But the bluegill has provided millions of largemouth with bite-sized forage.

If the predator bass takes it head first, and if his mouth is too small, seldom will the sunfish be able to 'back out'. But the bluegill has provided millions of largemouth with bite-sized forage.

Anglers in almost every state in the country have had opportunities to see huge bass chasing a bluegill across the surface of a lake or river. The bluegill exists in more waters than any other forage and is a particularly hearty breed. They are probably less sensitive to temperatures and oxygen extremes than any other sunfish.

The bluegill is also more tolerant of salt water than many forage fish. I was angling in a slough just off Florida's Apalachicola Bay. The brackish water contained several varieties of salt water species in addition to the largemouth and the bluegill. The 7 or 8 bass that I caught that day were not particularly memorable until I tossed a perch-colored Devil's Horse toward the dying ripples where a large bluegill had leaped from the water somewhat in haste. The seven pound largemouth that was chasing the sunfish exploded on my plug and was soon anchoring an impressive stringer.

The bluegill, or bream as he's sometimes known in southern circles, is found in all types of waters from the smallest creek to the largest reservoir. Its habitat ranges from weedlined shores to deep water pilings. Structure of any kind will attract the every-hungry bluegill. Freshwater shrimp that inhabit bogs of aquatic weeds, and small bugs that frequent logjams and fallen timber, are among its favorites.

Bluegills rely heavily on depth and cover to escape their predators, so nearby deep water is important. Like many sunfish, the bluegill will feed on the surface frequently, snacking on small bugs, minnows, larvae, and other tiny morsels that either feed on top or fall helplessly into the water. Bluegills generally start their spawn as largemouths are finishing up. Their timing is great.

Red Belly Rations

Bluegill and other sunfish, such as the redbreast and redear (or 'shellcracker') have been used for bait in many waters, but some states prohibit their use as bait. It is wise to check state regulations prior to using the 'real thing.'

The redbreast, like the bluegill, prefers a sandy bottom, however, it has a preference in water type, the flowing waters of a small river or creek. They seldom grow past a pound, so they remain of good forage size for the largemouth. Other species in the sunfish family such as the redear sunfish and the warmouth also remain bite-sized to bass for most of their lives.

Shallow water lures fished near heavy cover could not do better than to resemble a bluegill or redbreast. Several tackle manufacturers like Rebel and Bagley have been producing lures which look very authentic. Bass up to 14 pounds have been taken on the "naturalized" baits since their introduction.

Research is currently being performed on introducing bass fingerlings from Florida into some northern heated waters (via power plants) prior to the crappie spawn in that area. It is hoped that this stocking will enable the bass to grow and feed on the small crappie.

Succulent Specks

Crappie congregate immediately before and during spawning and provide many of the larger bass with some forage. Unfortunately, they spawn prior to the bass, and the small "speckled perch", as they are known in the south, grow quickly to a larger size than the bass fingerlings can effectively feed on.

Research is currently being done on the possibilities of introducing bass fingerlings from Florida into some northern heated waters (via power plants) prior to the crappie spawn in that area. It is hoped that this stocking will enable the bass to grow and feed on the small crappie.

Natural foods of the crappie are small minnows and freshwater shrimp which frequent weedy areas. Most aquatic plants house small shrimp and a productive bass lure around such places could be a crappie replica. In addition to the shallows, they feed in deeper waters beneath water hyacinths in the south, and hydrilla, which is now growing in some 30 states.

The crappie prefers larger waters to small creeks and canals and will school readily either in a suspended position or on structure. They are most susceptible as bass forage when they inhabit lily pads, submerged trees or bridges. When they move into deeper waters and suspend several feet above bottom they are less prone to attack from the structure-oriented bass.

Eating Their Own

Fingerling or small bass are also part of the diet of larger bass. From the second or third week of life on, the carnivorous largemouth will attempt to eat almost any other bass that is smaller than itself. Both the female and male spawning couple will even make meals of their own fry when they feel the urge. I once found a 10-inch bass in the protruding stomach of an eight pounder that I had caught on a cold, spring day.

The fact that the predator can also be forage should be clear from looking at length frequency charts of largemouth bass from fisheries biologists. A typical analysis of Lake Conroe in Texas found that 118 two-inch fingerlings per acre dwindled to a total of only 5 bass above 12-inches per acre just two years later. That time period is more than sufficient to allow growth of each bass to at least 12-inches and more, probably 15-inches.

Bass can't be used as bait, but plugs resembling them are certainly effective in the spring during and just after the spawn. The lures should be fished near the typical spawning areas and nearby cover that the bass inhabit. The bass is a member of the sunfish family and, as such, is fair game for larger bass predators.

Minnow Clan

Minnows native to the water being fished always make the best bait. They are the primary, natural food of many fish and bass are accustomed to feeding on them. Minnows of one variety or another are found in all waters that are unaffected by acid rain and the like. Over 200 species exist in North America, but only a dozen or so are numerous and large enough to be of consequence to bass fishermen.

Fatheads may be the most popular species among anglers in the states. They are also called tuffies, mud minnows and chubs. The hardiest of the minnow clan, they live in lakes and rivers and are seined in such areas to provide bait dealers with the bulk of their stock. Fatheads in the 2 to 3 inch size are commonly available in cold spring waters while smaller versions can be found along banks throughout the year. This specie of minnow which resembles the pike, is also raised commercially in stock tanks without predators.

Hornyhead chubs, also called redtails, are a hardy forage found in rocky rivers from the mountain states eastward. They have a lateral band that extends along their body to a tail spot. The creek chub is similar in appearance and also ranges east of the Rockies. The large minnows are lively and will jump over a seine when trapped by a bait 'prospector'. Other minnows of note, common to bait shops and predator bass, are the shiner group, the pearl dace, the finescale dace, the top minnows (mosquitofish and sailfin mollies), and the northern redbelly dace. Baitfish fingerlings would also include the popular madtoms, suckers, stonecats, yellow and white perch, and carp.

When buying minnows for use as bass bait, healthy bait will normally form a ball in one corner of the dealer's tank. Select from the congregation and keep them well supplied with oxygen while transferring them to the environment of the bass. Oxygen packed bags, tablets, or a good aerator should suffice. The adventurous can seine their own, right from the water being fished. Select the larger 3 or 4 inch sized minnows for best bass activity.

Egg-Loving Caledonian

Florida's Caledonian minnow, known also as a 'bullhead' although no relation to the catfish family, is an egg-lover and thus, is a super springtime bait for bass. In fact, it is a more palatable meal for smaller largemouth due to its smaller size. The endless game of the minnow darting into a bass nest to slurp up an egg breakfast and then being driven away or captured and removed bodily by the protective bass goes on for several weeks during the spawning season.

The Caledonian is range-limited but is a very productive bait. Its favorite habitat during the year is similar to that of the redhorse shiner, the club, the Brazos shiner, and other small minnows: eel grass and aquatic weeds in sloughs, small canals and creeks. Most of us have, at one time or another, seined some small waters and found multitudes of bait fish. And probably a game fish or two has also been captured on one of these bait seining trips. The relationship between the bass and its minnow forage can be apparent in a situation like this.

Whiskered Bullheads

A friend and I were working plastic worms along a shoreline in a cove off of the main body of a small southern lake when we noticed an unusual event. The shallows would erupt periodically with feeding bass, yet our boat's live well sure hadn't heard about it.

Finally, in desperation, we decided to inspect the battle-grounds regardless of whether or not we would 'spook' our quarry. As we approached the shore, dark clouds became visible in the partially stained water. Upon closer inspection, small, dark brown fish were discovered moving in and out from the bank in huge schools. Little bullhead catfish of about one-inch in length were being 'gorged on' by many small bass hanging just off of the shoreline.

Our tackle boxes held nothing suitable to match the forage that spring day, probably because the tackle manufacturers had yet to realize the importance of catfish as a bass forage. In Hawaii, bass have a distinct preference during summer and fall for Chinese catfish roughly 3 to 5 inches long, according to William Devick, Fish and Game Division Biologist. Although not abundant enough in many bass habitats to be a large component of the diet, they are the preferred live bait in Hawaii for catching bass.

In the northern midwest states, bullhead catfish comprise an important part of the bass forage intake. The most important fish consumed were the bluegill and brown bullhead, according to a Department of Natural Resources study on largemouth bass feeding habits in Wisconsin. Not an uncommon occurrence in many states, one wonders why more lure manufacturers don't produce a good replica.

Bullheads are scavengers. They are bottom feeders and can be found almost anywhere near the lake or creek bottom. They even move into the shallows during daylight hours with a hot sun directly overhead. Bullheads feed in schools and they can reproduce so many fry that the lake becomes overpopulated with them. When this happens, their growth will be stunted.

Regional Forage

Bass love to consume freshly-stocked cold water game fish such as salmon, trout, and even muskellunge, and this trait has led to changes in techniques used by many fish and game agencies when introducing them in waters containing bass. Such fish are not stocked as forage, but bass don't know that. The impact of the rainbow trout-painted crank baits in the state of California is well known.

Smelt, during spawning season in the upper northeastern states, are a part of bass intake. Fisheries biologists in Maine have even found bass adapting their feeding habits to this forage on into the summer. "Within the first two weeks of June, I have captured largemouth bass which were feeding on smelts at a depth of 40 feet," says J. Dennis McNeish of Maine's Inland Fisheries and Wildlife Department. "The lake is newly established and has a highly abundant smelt population."

Many anglers in the northeastern states also find the anadromous alewife in stomach analyses of the bass during late spring and early summer. The bass sometimes gorge themselves on fingerling alewiles in the one to three inch size range which are so tremendously abundant that time of year.

The sea run, herring-like fish ascend coastal streams to fresh water seeking ponds in which to spawn. The young remain there until they are at least two inches long before migrating to sea, usually in the late summer. While growing in the ponds, the young alewiles provide a short term forage base much higher than the pond could support over a longer period.

Several northeast states are currently studying the bass-alewife relationship. While many studies have found the alewife to be an important food item for bass, Pennsylvania's, on the contrary, have not. "It was hoped and assumed that the largemouths would feed on them," states Charles Cooper of the Pennsylvania Division of Fisheries, "but stomach content analyses showed that our hopes were denied."

Secret Forage

Brackish water bass adapt to other forage fish from the sea as well as the freshwater forage that may exist. Although many marine fish can outswim the largemouth, he'll get his share of the smaller prey. A friend in Melbourne, Florida had been impressing many anglers with his consistent catches of 10-pound bass and I had to find out his secret.

He made me swear not to tell a soul, but I think after 15 years or so, the statute of limitations has run out. I'm sure that it would be okay if I only told you what his highly successful bait was. He used small 6 to 8-inch mullet to entice those huge Florida bass. A cast net was used to catch his bait from small sloughs and bay inlets. The fish were even able to tolerate freshwater for a couple of hours while on the hook.

World Record Food

Forage of the next world record largemouth? It may just be the dormillon. It is a natural food fish for black bass in Honduras. Lake Yojoa is 8 miles wide at its widest point and stretches 14 miles in length. Its depth averages 30 feet and reaches down to 85 in some areas. Yojoa's forage-filled shoreline is maiden cane and bullrushes with lily pads interspersed in two to seven feet of water. Eel grass covers the shallows down to about 15 feet and its length, at times approaching four feet, harbors abundant dormillon forage.

The lake is one to two million years old and was created by volcanic eruptions which sealed a canyon, forming a dam at, what is now, the north end of the lake. A few thousand years ago, sinkholes developed in the natural lake's limestone and coquina rock floor and drained the lake. The three streams which flow into the lake were still present, but the lake bed was dry.

The Mayan Indians then built a city on the dry lake bed, and since then, the sinkholes have been clogged up and the lake filled to its normal capacity. Today, these 2,000 year old Mayan ruins lie beneath the surface, in seventy feet of water. Besides being able to catch bass from submerged ancient Mayan temples, an angler will find that this may be the only bass lake in the world where he can look up and see monkeys swinging in the trees.

When live bait fishing with dormillon, the small four or five inch size is often used. At the daily noon break, guides take a monofilament hand-line, a piece of worm, and catch a gallon can full of the bait fish. Several anglers have tried dormillon and caught some good bass from those waters, but not the world record, yet.

Approximate Range Of The Tilapia

This species of forage is becoming more prominent in the diets of bass as their range and numbers spread. The import was introduced into the states in the fifties for research purposes. Tilapia nilotica, a noted game fish and food fish, and its cousin Tilapia aurea (blue tilapia) which is more aggressive, prolific, and, as a result, extremely difficult to control, are now dispersed in several states.

The forage resembles a bluegill in size and general appearance, and without adequate control, the species is capable of displacing more desirable game and food fish. Highly fertile, power plant lakes in the south have been very conducive to the species and also to their predators thus far. The range of the tilapia would be expected to move northward, limited primarily by wintertime water temperatures.

BASS SERIES LIBRARY!

Six Great Books With A Wealth Of Information For Bass Fishermen

By Larry Larsen

I. FOLLOW THE FORAGE FOR BETTER BASS ANGLING - VOL. 1
BASS/PREY RELATIONSHIP - The most important key to catching bass is finding them in a feeding mood. Knowing the predominant forage, its activity and availability, as well as its location in a body of water will enable an angler to catch more and larger bass. Whether you fish artificial lures or live bait, you will benefit from this book.

SPECIAL FEATURES
- PREDATOR/FORAGE INTERACTION
- BASS FEEDING BEHAVIOR
- UNDERSTANDING BASS FORAGE
- BASS/PREY PREFERENCES
- FORAGE ACTIVITY CHART

II. FOLLOW THE FORAGE FOR BETTER BASS ANGLING -VOL. 2

TECHNIQUES - Beginners and veterans alike will achieve more success utilizing proven concepts that are based on predator/forage interactions. Understanding the reasons behind lure or bait success will result in highly productive, bass-catching patterns.

SPECIAL FEATURES
- LURE SELECTION CRITERIA
- EFFECTIVE PATTERN DEVELOPMENT
- NEW BASS CATCHING TACTICS
- FORAGING HABITAT
- BAIT AND LURE METHODS

III. BASS PRO STRATEGIES

- Professional fishermen have opportunities to devote extended amounts of time to analyzing a body of water and planning a productive day on it. They know how changes in pH, water temperature, color and fluctuations affect bass fishing, and they know how to adapt to weather and topographical variations. This book reveals the methods that the country's most successful tournament anglers have employed to catch bass almost every time out. The reader's productivity should improve after spending a few hours with this compilation of techniques!

SPECIAL FEATURES
- MAPPING & WATER ELIMINATION
- LOCATE DEEP & SHALLOW BASS
- BOAT POSITION FACTORS
- WATER CHEMISTRY INFLUENCES
- TOPOGRAPHICAL TECHNIQUES

IV. BASS LURES - TRICKS & TECHNIQUES

- Modifications of lures and development of new baits and techniques continue to keep the fare fresh, and that's important. Bass seem to become "accustomed" to the same artificials and presentations seen over and over again. As a result, they become harder to catch. It's the new approach that again sparks the interest of some largemouth. To that end, this book explores some of the latest ideas for modifying, rigging and using them. The lure modifications, tricks and techniques presented within these covers will work anywhere in the country.

SPECIAL FEATURES
- UNIQUE LURE MODIFICATIONS
- IN-DEPTH VARIABLE REASONING
- PRODUCTIVE PRESENTATIONS
- EFFECTIVE NEW RIGGINGS
- TECHNOLOGICAL ADVANCES

V. SHALLOW WATER BASS - Catching shallow water largemouth is not particularly difficult. Catching lots of them usually is. Even more challenging is catching lunker-size bass in seasons other than during the spring spawn. Anglers applying the information within the covers of this book on marshes, estuaries, reservoirs, lakes, creeks or small ponds should triple their results. The book details productive new tactics to apply to thin-water angling. Numerous photographs and figures easily define the optimal locations and proven methods to catch bass.

SPECIAL FEATURES
- UNDERSTANDING BASS/COVER INTERFACE
- METHODS TO LOCATE BASS CONCENTRATIONS
- ANALYSIS OF WATER TYPES
- TACTICS FOR SPECIFIC HABITATS
- LARSEN'S "FLORA FACTOR"

VI. BASS FISHING FACTS - This angler's guide to the lifestyles and behavior of the black bass is a reference source of sorts, never before compiled. The book explores the behavior of bass during pre- and post-spawn as well as during bedding season. It examines how bass utilize their senses to feed and how they respond to environmental factors. The book details how fishermen can be more productive by applying such knowledge to their bass angling. The information within the covers of this book includes those bass species, known as "other" bass, such as redeye, Suwannee, spotted, etc.

SPECIAL FEATURES
- BASS FORAGING MOTIVATORS
- DETAILED SPRING MOVEMENTS
- A LOOK AT BASS SENSES
- GENETIC INTRODUCTION/STUDIES
- MINOR BASS SPECIES & HABITATS

Breinigsville, PA USA
25 June 2010
240552BV00004B/2/P